CRIMSON SEEDS
EIGHTEEN PIME MARTYRS

D1468252

CRIMSON SEEDS

EIGHTEEN PIME MARTYRS

Mariagrazia Zambon

Translated from the Italian (*A Causa di Gesù, Diciotto Missionari Martiri del PIME*. Bologna: EMI. 1994) by Father Steve Baumbusch, PIME

PIME
WORLD
PRESS

Detroit, Michigan

From the Translator

"The blood of martyrs is the seed of faith"

The translation of *A Causa di Gesù* has proven to be a true labor of love for me. As I became more and more familiar with the stories of P.I.M.E.'s 18 martyrs, I found myself awestruck by the simple but heroic witness of each one, amazed by their spirit of generosity and self-sacrifice, inspired by their love for God and their people, encouraged by the obvious presence of the Lord in all their struggles. In short, my own faith has been strengthened in the process.

Is this what it means to say that the blood of martyrs is the seed of faith? Not only the spread of the faith among non-Christians, but also the blossoming and growth of faith among us who strive to live out our Christian calling every day? I think so, and I pray that the *"crimson seeds"* of the P.I.M.E. martyrs may find fertile ground in all who read this book.

Special thanks go out to Mr. Paul Witte for his editing and proofreading and to Mrs. Margaret Fleming for layout.

I offer this translation especially for the P.I.M.E. seminarians in formation, that they may know the rich heritage with which the Lord has blessed our community and be inspired to give of themselves totally in responding to God's call.

Fr. Steve Baumbusch, PIME
Easter, 1997

PIME World Press
17330 Quincy St.
Detroit, Michigan 48221-2765

Printed in U.S.A.
Library of Congress Catalog Card Number: 97-67638
ISBN: 0-9642010-4-6

CONTENTS

BURMA: LAND OF MYSTERY AND INTRIGUE

BANGLADESH: THE UNKNOWN COUNTRY

THE PHILIPPINES: A DIALOGUE
OF MANY VOICES

AFTERWORD:
MARTYRDOM IN THE LIGHT
OF THE GOSPEL

ABBREVIATIONS

"Fr." ("Frs." in the plural) is the abbreviation used throughout the book for the priestly title, "Father" ("Fathers"). "Br." ("Brs.") is used for "Brother" ("Brothers"), the title of an unordained member of a religious order or society.

P.I.M.E. stands for "Pontifical Institute for Foreign Missions" in Latin.

FORWARD

By Fr. Franco Cagnasso, PIME

WORDS FOR OUR TIME?

"MARTYR," "MARTYRDOM": FOR MANY, THESE WORDS HAVE THE flavor of the past, of a mentality distant from our own time, which rejects romanticism and useless heroism. Talk of "martyrdom" for one's country or faith seems to be a remnant of another era, when people were still naive enough to believe that it was worthwhile to sacrifice something, even one's life, for an ideal.

Or, for believers, these words have the flavor of heroism. The church has always declared boldly that "the blood of martyrs is the seed of the faith."

But when you receive word that your friend, a missionary in the Philippines, has been shot to death as he was returning home by car, you feel neither the flavor of past times nor that of heroism: you feel only a great emptiness and immense sadness.

In martyrdom, all the suffering, injustice, cruelty and death of humanity appear in a very immediate and concrete way. If there are martyrs it is because there are people who are fiercely intolerant of others, powerful and violent people who do not respect freedom, goodness, and truth. If there are martyrs, it is because there are oppressors who think nothing of torture and murder; there are cowards who attack from hiding and then flee.

What remains, then, is blood and fear, the suffering of those who were loved by the one killed, and bewilderment and anger over the fact that once more evil has triumphed.

It would be wonderful if, following every martyrdom, the persecutors were converted, the oppressed were renewed in courage, and throngs of followers were ready to take the martyr's place; but that's not always the case.

The persecution of the Roman Empire lasted for centuries; so too in many other times and places, martyrdom has been carried out in bloodshed, in dank prison cells, in anguished acts of conscience, without any fruit in sight for generations to come. Hope, faith, and reconciliation have been most difficult to maintain.

No, we don't like these words. They contradict everything for which we work and struggle: respect, peace, justice, mutual love, the acceptance of Christ. We prefer that they would be forgotten, buried in a distant and irretrievable past.

But is that possible? Is it possible to close our eyes or block our ears to a world which is still, just as much as in the past, continually subject to upheavals of violence, infected by disguised corruptions of the truth, threatened by the malicious and unscrupulous?

How can we ignore the fact that so many are still waiting to hear what Jesus announced in the synagogue of Nazareth? "The Spirit has sent me to announce good news to the poor, to proclaim liberty to captives and sight to the blind, to free the oppressed, and to proclaim a year of favor from the Lord." (Lk. 4:18-19)

On hearing these words, "all of those in the synagogue were filled with indignation" (v. 28), and they began to pour out upon Jesus, meek and humble of heart, the hostility, suspicion, and rejection which would accompany His mission right up to His condemnation and death on the cross.

The absurdity of martyrdom is that there is no sense of proportion. It does not arise out of a struggle for power, nor from a military engagement to acquire land and wealth, nor from a confrontation between equally armed forces.

On the one side, there is Pilate, who can rightly claim: "I have the power to release you and the power to crucify you." (Jn. 19:10) On the other side there is Jesus, who does not want anyone to wield a sword (Jn. 18:11) and who uses nothing but the power of the truth.

So today, on the one side are violent fanatics and mercenaries who attack from the shadows, without the courage to look their victims in the eye; and on the other side is Fr. Carzedda, a meek and humble man of dialogue, who could serenely reveal to others the motivation for his commitment, his way of following Jesus.

You see, martyrs are not super-strong; nor do they despise their own lives in the name of some cause. They are not obstinate, ready to risk everything just to be proved right; nor do they think they won when they've really lost because of relying too much on themselves. These kinds of people are at first feared by the world, then admired if they win and despised if they lose.

But martyrs, for most people, are difficult to understand.

Jesus knew what it meant to struggle against terrible forces and to do so with the most illogical of weapons. When He wanted to illustrate to His disciples what their mission would be like, He chose an image which needs no further comment: "I am sending you like sheep among wolves." (Mt. 10:16)

Does it surprise or scandalize us if a pack of wolves attacks and devours a sheep? The scandal is, more than anything else, that someone would send the sheep among the wolves, that the weapons of evangelization are always and only truth, meekness, and visible love.

We don't like to speak of martyrdom, but we cannot do less than to expect it and even, for those who have the grace, to desire it, because this is the road traveled by Jesus, a road which each generation must embark upon anew.

Christ is present in all of those who are victims, because He has taken upon Himself every suffering and sin. The innocents massacred in Rwanda, the street children murdered in Rio de Janeiro, the kids forced into prostitution in Bangkok, those eliminated through ethnic cleansing in the Balkans: all of these are being crucified in the world today.

The disciple accepts becoming a victim so that the world will know that Jesus is truly the only path to salvation, so that even today people will hear the message that Christ is present and that it is worthwhile to follow Him: yes, even at the cost of one's life.

Martyrdom is a moment of the highest truth.

"Those who do evil hate the light; they do not come near it for fear their deeds will be exposed." (Jn. 3:20) The faithful follower of Jesus is hated and attracts the anger of those who do evil camouflaged as good, perhaps passed off as something done for the benefit of the people, the nation, or the will of God.

In martyrdom, this evil is forced out into the open, to angry confrontation with the light, to explicit refutation of the Gospel of love. And at the same time, in martyrdom, Christ once again reveals Himself in strong opposition to the world; this time His only weapons are the faith of His disciples and the patience of those who love.

The oppressors think they have won, but the ones who suffer know that they are never alone. Martyrs are not bound by time. They were incomprehensible 2,000 years ago and they are incomprehensible today. They were and are necessary, precisely because they go beyond the criteria and calculations of the wise. "The one who loses his life for my sake and for the Gospel's will preserve it." (Mk. 9:35)

To the one who believes only what can be seen, touched, and possessed; to the one steeped in the idolatry of self or one's own ideology, the martyrs respond that their power is God, the God of life and pardon, and that the rock upon which they are built is Christ. The madness which is so afraid of losing and which spreads oppression and terror, is confronted with the peaceful murmur of living water which is poured forth from the martyr as a gift of the Spirit: the logic of truth and love which no fire can overcome and no arms can destroy.

So, we must indeed speak of martyrdom, and I wish I knew how to do so without rhetoric and only with great faith.

We begin with the martyrdom of Jesus: the cross is not a plaster statue to hang on our walls, but rather a horrible, revolting instrument of torture; Jesus was so afraid of it that He sweat blood at the thought.

The martyrs of today are afraid as well. They are assailed by anguish in the monotony of a life in prison, in the uncertainty of waiting for judgment, in the fear that an assassin might be around the next corner. They are assailed by doubts. Should I stay as a testimony to my people? Or should I leave so that I do not cause them even more trouble and suffering? Alberic Crescitelli was captured when, after risking so much with his people, he was trying to get away so as not to put them in greater danger!

The martyrs of today also see their flock being dispersed, their projects destroyed, their lives come to nothing, and they too cry out: "My God, why have you abandoned me?" (Mt. 27:46)

But it must be this way, until the end of time. There must be those who make this cry together with Jesus, in the name of all those who seem abandoned by God, all those who are tread upon by others, all those who are destroyed, "like sheep led to the slaughter." (Acts 8:32) There must be those who do not renounce their humanity which has been saved by the Lord, and do not deny the Father but abandon themselves to Him.

Then, what remains is blood, silence, and sadness.

But from the grave, with many rocks rolled against it to put an end to the dangerous "fable" of a God who comes to earth, life bursts forth once again.

The church has existed for 2,000 years because, in spite of her errors and sins and notwithstanding even the fact that many of her own members have killed and made martyrs, she has never ceased to be nourished by this new life. Even in the midst of a thousand compromises, the faith continues firmly that our existence is rooted in God, that we will never be saved by trading the truth for our lives. Rather, we are saved by boldly proclaiming it, because it is Christ Himself.

In the almost 150 years since its foundation, 18 P.I.M.E. missionaries have suffered sudden and violent deaths: two in the first 92 years and sixteen in the last 52 years. This fact makes you stop and think. It wakes you up a bit to the possibility that perhaps we have been viewing or presenting the missionary vocation of today as somewhat watered down, comfortable, or compromised.

"Blessed will be that day when I will be asked to suffer much for Your Gospel, but how much more blessed the day when I shall be found worthy to shed my blood for it." These are the words recited by P.I.M.E. missionaries when they receive their mission cross during their departure ceremony.

May the Lord grant that we continue to believe and live these words, for ourselves and for all the disciples who are made martyrs by our time, for all the little ones whom the idolatry of every age crushes and kills.

MARTYRDOM IS ALWAYS GOD'S DESIGN

"Martyrdom is never a human plan," Archbishop Thomas Becket says in T. S. Eliot's play *Murder in the Cathedral.*

It's Christmas, 1170. During the morning sermon the Archbishop, having just returned to England, calmly and clearly reveals his spiritual conflict in the face of his imminent death and the possibility of martyrdom which confronts him. Doubt torments him, possibly leading him to be tempted toward pride and the ambition of eternal glory. But it gives way to the sole desire to place himself once again entirely in the will of God.

Just four days later he is murdered in the cathedral of Canterbury by four of Henry II's soldiers.

> My dear children, let us not think of a martyr as simply a good Christian who has been killed because he is a Christian. This would only lead to sadness. Neither do we think of a martyr simply as a good Christian who has been chosen to join the company of the saints. This would lead us only to rejoicing. Our sadness and our rejoicing is never like that of the world.
>
> Christian martyrdom does not happen by chance, just as one does not become a saint by chance. In fact, Christian martyrdom is even less a result of human will than is becoming a saint, because one can always become a leader of others by force of will or some manipulation.
>
> Martyrdom is always God's design, flowing out of His love for His people, to gather and guide them, to lead them back along His way. It is never a human plan, because the true martyr is one who has become

an instrument of God, who has given up his own will for the will of God, and who does not desire anything for himself, not even the glory of martyrdom.

Thus, while the church on earth weeps and rejoices at the same time in a way the world cannot understand, in paradise the saints have been exalted on high, because here on earth they have been brought very low; and they are to be considered, not as we see them, but in the light of the Divine from whom they draw their very being.

Thomas Stern Eliot

OCEANIA:
A DANGEROUS
PARADISE

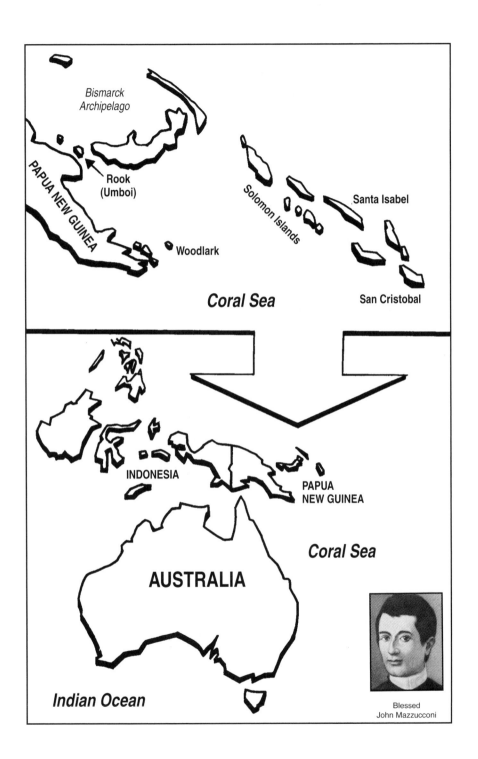

Bismarck
Archipelago

PAPUA NEW GUINEA

Rook
(Umboi)

Solomon Islands

Santa Isabel

Woodlark

San Cristobal

Coral Sea

INDONESIA

PAPUA
NEW GUINEA

Coral Sea

AUSTRALIA

Indian Ocean

Blessed
John Mazzucconi

INTRODUCTION

By Mariagrazia Zambon

WHEN THE FIRST MISSIONARIES FROM THE MILAN SEMINARY FOR Foreign Missions, the precursor of P.I.M.E., arrived at Woodlark and Rook (now known as Umboi Island) in the autumn of 1852, they were among the first white men to set foot on these two islands, having been preceded only by the Marist missionaries, who landed on Woodlark in 1847 and on Rook in 1848. In fact, these two islands, which are part of a network of 10,000 islands, had hardly been explored at all.

Woodlark, an extension of a submerged peninsula which connects to New Guinea, was discovered in 1832 by a certain Captain Grimes, of the whaling ship, *Woodlark*, from which the island takes its name. Just four years later, the first British arrived, but the first to make direct contact with the natives were the French Marists. Far from the shipping routes, and thus from commercial interest, the island remained unknown for a long time, until Fr. Carlo Salerio, a missionary from Milan and friend of Mazzucconi, drew the first detailed map of the coastline and the features of the interior.

The island of Rook, 600 leagues east of Woodlark, between New Guinea and New Brittany, seems instead to be among the first discovered by the Europeans; Captain Menez, a Spaniard, landed there in 1537, but then it was forgotten.

The Apostolic Vicariate of Melanesia, to which Woodlark and Rook belonged, also contained New Guinea, the Solomons, New Ireland, New Britain, and many smaller islands. The first bishop of this immense Pacific mission was Bishop Epalle, who landed on the island of San Cristobal in the Solomons, on December 1, 1845 with seven fathers and six brothers of the Marist congregation. Eleven days later, sailing north, he reached Isabel island, which he made the center of the mission. On the sixteenth of the same month, heedless of the many reports about the temperament of these islanders, he took to land with two fathers, a brother, two sailors, and the captain — all unarmed. As soon as they tried to communicate with the natives, they were attacked, with the bishop and the captain being killed. The survivors returned to San Cristobal. But here too the mission did not have a happy ending. In 1847, one of the missionaries died of a fever, and the other three were massacred by the natives.

Bishop Collomb, successor of Bishop Epalle, decided to abandon the Solomons temporarily, and tried to open a new mission at Woodlark, about which he had received favorable reports. He landed there in 1847. But this island was no heaven on earth either. In fact, when the French missionaries landed, they found the people to be very closed and primitive: "We could never discover," writes Fr. Reina a few years later, describing a situation identical to that faced by the French missionaries, "whether they have an idea of God more or less like our own."

> They have a firm belief in a spirit that goes by the general name of *Marcaba*. He eats their pigs, kills any men that he meets, and enters the villages at night to knock on the doors of their houses; he is driven away by curses. He is the cause of diseases. Some say he has a body, painted in a monstrous way; others claim that he is not a physical being at all. There are also those who say that he speaks with a whistle, and any strange or unusual sound is generally considered to be the voice of *Marcaba*. A bad person is also called a *Marcaba*.

To battle and control the forces of nature, they practice magic. Fr. Carlo Salerio wrote,

> [Magic] represents for the savage a particular aspect of reality which is strictly connected to every important

fact of life. Human existence from birth to death (and beyond) is presented to the savages in a magical, animistic atmosphere, thus in a dynamic of diverse influences, which they adore and despise in turn, seeking to maintain a balance of contrasting forces, a balance which is always in danger. Magic is also closely linked to their economic life. In any kind of adversity or important enterprise whose results are uncertain with mere human means, magic is considered a necessity. The natives make use of it in the cultivation of their gardens, in fishing, in the construction of their longboats, in the invocation of winds and weather, in questions of romance and when they want protection from danger or assurance of success, when they want to protect their own health or cause some infirmity to an enemy. They have prayers and incantations for everything.

At first, the arrival of the French missionaries had a positive effect. In fact, they succeeded in putting an end to the bloody tribal warfare which often brought about the destruction of whole villages. This occurred because the missionaries were able to win the good graces of the people through the distribution of iron products (needles, saws, pots and pans), since metal was unknown in the islands. Unfortunately, beyond this purely utilitarian interest, the missionaries did not succeed in establishing a good relationship with the people. Not only did they explicitly reject the Gospel message, they also despised anything that was different from their traditions and culture.

In the meantime the missionaries once again attempted to expand to other islands, and Bishop Collomb landed with a few confreres on Rook. They were there no longer than two months, however, when the young bishop was stricken by fever and an intestinal disease, and died. The survivors returned to Woodlark and the superiors decided to abandon the project.

In June of 1848 the Congregation for the Propagation of the

Faith began to look for an institute which would accept such a dangerous challenge. The Barnabites declined, as did the Picpusians and the Oblates of Mary Immaculate. Only the missionaries of the Milan Seminary for Foreign Missions, seeking their very first field of work, accepted. The expedition, composed of seven young missionaries led by Fr. Paolo Reina, sailed from London on Holy Saturday of 1852, and reached the island of Rook on October 28 of the same year, going on from there to Woodlark.

But right away the difficulties and lack of understanding that had plagued the earlier attempts of the Marists appeared again. The missionaries were considered to be some kind of enchanters, and were blamed for any misfortunes which took place on the island. According to the village chieftain, disease and famine were the result of the missionaries' condemnation of immoral practices (especially in regard to sex) and their admonitions. "We could not even assist the sick," wrote Fr. Reina, "because if we gave them medicine, they would say that our magic was good or bad, according to the effect of the medicine, to which they say we have transmitted our own power."

By the beginning of 1855, all the natives had deserted the mission of Woodlark. Thefts began to occur. At night crops were burnt. The missionaries were threatened and insulted. Day after day the missionaries experienced their mission failing. Thus, after less than three years, in the spring of 1855, the Italian missionaries withdrew from these two islands as well, without any visible results. Of the seven who left Italy in good health, Br. Corti died of a fever on Rook, Fr. Mazzucconi was killed on Woodlark, Fr. Reina fell seriously ill and died in Italy in 1861, and Br. Tacchini had a nervous breakdown from the struggles he endured. Only three survived intact: Fr. Ambrosoli, who remained in Sydney and died in 1891; Fr. Raimondi, who became the bishop of Hong Kong; and Fr. Salerio, who returned to Italy and founded the congregation of the Reparation Sisters of Nazareth.

Woodlark, after the attempts of the Marists (1847–52) and of the Milan Seminary for the Foreign Missions (1852–55), was abandoned.

After a long absence, P.I.M.E. returned to Papua New Guinea in 1980, on the island of Goodenough (Diocese of Alotau), at Bolu Bolu and Wataluma. In 1986–87, Bishop Desmond Moore also entrusted to P.I.M.E. the Trobriand Islands, a parish comprised of boundless ocean, extending up to the small archipelago of Woodlark. Even today, Woodlark itself does not enjoy the stable presence of a priest, and things have not changed much since the days of Mazzucconi. There are still difficulties in communicating, inaccessible areas, hostility and indifference from many groups of the natives, who have remained isolated from the rest of the world. The spiritualism at the base of many traditional cults still leaves its traces in the mentality of Christian converts (about 50 out of 2,400 inhabitants).

The mission in Oceania, then, remains an incredible challenge for all the missionary priests, sisters, and lay people who work there.

BLESSED JOHN MAZZUCCONI
(MARCH 1, 1826 – SEPTEMBER, 1855)

It is the summer of 1845. A small group of seminarians have organized
a trip to the Carthusian monastery in Pavia. Among them are John
Mazzucconi and his friend Carlo Salerio. They stay there for a few
days, and after admiring the splendid art work in this place of quiet
and prayer, they have the opportunity to meet and speak with the
prior, Fr. Suprier, who has become a monk after having served as a missionary in India. He tells the young men about his desire to see a seminary established in Italy for the foreign missions. He talks about his life
in India, the experiences he had and the people he met, the good that
he accomplished and received. The seminarians are fascinated and full
of admiration, especially John and Carlo. Thus, after returning to the
seminary of St. Peter the Martyr in Monza, they begin a frequent correspondence with the prior.

"How is it that in Italy there is not already an institute to prepare
priests who want to go the missions?" Fr. Suprier would ask; and his
words reverberate in the hearts of those young men, who feel as if they
are addressed to them personally. John begins to cultivate this dream
for himself, and in order to take the first steps, he studies foreign languages: English, which he has already been studying for some time, as
well as French and German. He never speaks to his classmates about
his missionary vocation, though, for fear of being misunderstood. Instead, he confides in his spiritual director, from whom he receives the
dry response: "Are you crazy? Your India is here!" It is a heavy blow, but
he is not discouraged. Rather, after a ten-day retreat with Fr. Suprier in
1846, his decision is reinforced. Yet he must wait, not only for priestly

ordination, but also for the establishment of the first Italian missionary institute, in Milan. In fact, Angelo Ramazzotti, a lawyer who left the bar to become a priest of the Oblates of Rho, has for some time held an active and lively interest in the missions.

In November of 1847, the Apostolic Delegate of Switzerland, Bishop Luquet, arrives in Milan from Rome, with the charge to communicate to the bishops of Lombardy Pope Pius IX's desire for a missionary institute to be established in Milan. With the blessing and support of the pope, Ramazzotti, newly named superior of the Oblates, does not hesitate. He commits himself personally to the realization of this project.

However, the events of 1848, especially the famous "five days of Milan," force the suspension of all initiatives.

The theological seminary of Milan, where John Mazzucconi is studying, is closed, and the seminarians are organized into teams to assist the refugees, the sick, and the wounded. John is among the most active in this work of charity. But when many of the seminarians, including Carlo Salerio, sign up for the student battalion of Lombardy to assist the troops of Carlo Alberto in resisting the Austrian attack on Mantua, Mazzucconi prefers to retire to his parents' home in order to continue his studies on his own.

Violence, patriotic furor, and the horrendous chaos of rifle and bayonet are not for him. He prefers to return temporarily to his village, Rancio, on the slopes of Lecco, where he was born on March 1, 1826 and where his large family still lives. There he studies, prays, helps out at the parish, and waits for the reopening of the seminary.

Finally, in the summer of 1849, the Austrian police restore the structures confiscated from the diocese, which can now resume normal pastoral activity. The plans for establishing a seminary for the missions can move forward as well.[1] The first superior and director is Bishop Giuseppe Marinoni, called to substitute for Ramazzotti, who has been named the Bishop of Pavia.

---

[1] The official act of the foundation of the Lombardy Seminary for the Missions was signed by the bishops of Lombardy on December 1, 1850.

And so, when John Mazzucconi becomes a deacon in March of 1850, he requests to be admitted to the new seminary. His dream, and that of some of his friends, is finally realized.

He is ordained a priest on May 25. Two months later he receives a letter from Bishop Ramazzotti, inviting him to participate in the inauguration of the new "missionary seminary," which will be located at Ramazzotti's family home in Saronno. Thus, beginning on July 31, 1850, John Mazzucconi, Carlo Salerio, three other priests and two catechists, together with the rector and founder, Bishop Ramazzotti, begin this new adventure.

It is with the Bishop, waiting for his installation in the diocese of Pavia, that the first students engage in community life. "We pray, we study, we laugh," Mazzucconi relates in a letter, describing the family atmosphere in which everything is shared, discussed, and decided in common. Together, they write and edit the rule, or constitution, of the new institute. Together, they prepare for their mission departure by prayer, study, and charitable activities, adopting the missionary spirit of moderation and sacrifice. Together, from the very beginning, they begin to dream of going to Oceania.

They know that this immense continent, spread over the infinite surface of the Pacific Ocean, represents virgin territory and a difficult mission. This becomes the definitive criteria for their choice. In fact, in the rule of 1886 it is written: "The Institute, from its very beginning, will attempt to have its own missions among the most neglected and primitive of peoples." They are also aware that the Marists have requested permission to leave the mission of Melanesia-Micronesia, because of the difficulties they have encountered and because they are already committed in other parts of the Pacific Ocean.

On December 2, 1851, after months of agonized waiting, a letter from Cardinal Fransoni of the Congregation for the Propagation of the Faith arrives in Milan, where the Seminary for Foreign Missions has transferred. It gives the official assignment of the mission field: Melanesia-Micronesia.

Three and a half months later, on March 16, 1852, the Archbishop of Milan presents mission crosses to Frs. Paolo Reina (leader of the expedition), John Mazzucconi, Carlo Salerio, Timeoleone Raimondi, Angelo Ambrosoli, and the catechists, Brs. Giuseppe Corti and Luigi Tacchini. At noon on Holy Saturday of the same year, they sail from London:

> Within a few hours, we will be far from land … there will be nothing between us and the sea's abyss but a piece of wood... I hope that it stays like this for four or five months, always unstable and suspended between heaven and the abyss; I would like that very much. It will give me the correct idea of God's greatness which extends throughout infinity, and of His goodness which watches over a poor boat seeking its port. I will know in a special way what it means to be in the hands of God, and in God's hands, I will be safe...

John boards the *Tartaro*, a strong and fast ship, capable of holding 130 people. A little before departure John writes:

> Just for fun, there are also 400 other creatures, alive and happy: a bunch of chickens, roosters, and other two-legged animals, as well as pigs and sheep; for milk, there is also a heifer. When they all begin to sing, each in its own manner, we start to think that we are on solid ground, in the barnyard of some wealthy farmer, and not on a ship at sea.

Mazzucconi and his companions sail on this ship for three and half months before finally reaching Sydney, Australia. In the calm evenings, John loves to sit in a corner of the deck like "a philosopher or hermit" contemplating the sea:

> The magnificent spectacle of the sunset, the immensity of the calm ocean, especially the brilliant sky below the equator during the new moon, the flaming phosphorescence of the sea — it's amazing how much peace constantly abides in the vastness of this part of the

world; it seems that God alone reigns here, and His kingdom is one of peace.

During the long voyage, however, there were also moments in which the passengers feel that they have been forgotten by God, such as May 23, 1852 when, while rounding the Cape of Good Hope, the *Tartaro* barely missed colliding with another ship. Or another time, a month later, when a storm struck so violently that water was coming into the gangways and cabins. But finally, calm is restored.

> We go out onto the deck. The day has become calm and the sea more tranquil. I can't describe to you what it's like to see the sun shining on the ruins of a ship which is little more than a wreck: to see the ropes and spars and pulleys which had been flying through the air now laying still and lifeless on the deck. It is a spectacle that touches you, which truly makes you feel good; and to tell you the truth, I wish that many others would experience it. You feel like you are in the hands of God, as if with a breath, He could disperse the best laid plans...There's nothing left to do but thank God, who has spared us in our weakness and who has given us enough reason to believe that He will always save us; and to pray that His mercy toward us might continue.

On the morning of July 25, the coast of Australia comes into view and on the following day a battered *Tartaro* drops anchor in the port of Sydney. But the journey of the seven missionaries is not finished. They spend two months in the house of the Marists, where they study the language and customs of the inhabitants of the islands to which they are destined. Then they set sail once again, this time for Woodlark and Rook.

On the French schooner *Jeune Lucie* thoughts race and emotions run high. To the seven young missionaries it seems like dreaming with their eyes open. Finally it appears over the horizon: the outline of the island which, little by little, becomes more distinct. Cliffs overlooking the sea alternate with beaches of fine sand, and an endless line of mangroves, bougainvilleas, and orchids. A dense undergrowth of plants closes off the way to the mountainous, forest covered interior. A true "paradise on earth."

However, the spectacular barrier reefs, which are evidenced here and there in the intense blue of the ocean by lines of sparkling foam, represent a great danger for ships.

In Woodlark, the party splits up: Frs. Salerio and Raimondi, with one catechist, remain on the island, while Frs. Reina, Ambrosoli and Mazzucconi, with the other catechist and a Marist priest accompanying them, head for the island of Rook, which they reach on October 28, 1852. It is here that Fr. John will work for two and a half years.

On Woodlark the missionaries find some houses already built, but in Rook there is only a ruined hovel built by the Marists during their year of work there (1847–48). It is separated into rooms by walls made of tree bark and a horizontal latticework divides the hovel into two floors: living quarters below and storage above. The roof is covered with tiles made of ironwood, but it is in such bad shape that when it rains the water comes in everywhere. Scorpions, serpents and insects enter at will through the holes in the walls.

Mazzucconi, however, never complains in his letters about the material conditions of his life. The habit of self-sacrifice makes it easier to accept a situation that for us would be almost intolerable: total isolation for a year and sometimes more (just once a year a rented boat arrives from Sydney with mail and supplies of food and medicine), the constant hot and humid weather, thousands of mosquitoes and other insects, the poor food consisting mostly of taro root, from which a flour similar to tapioca is drawn.

Contrary to what the missionaries in Woodlark are doing, those in Rook choose the path of indirect evangelization: "For now," Mazzucconi writes, "the mission needs to consist in being constantly in touch with the local people and learning their language; then, when God wills, we will speak to them about Him." The missionaries do everything they can to help the islanders improve their living conditions: they teach them to use mortar and bricks, to work with iron and use the wheel, they introduce new plants with seeds imported from Australia (corn, oranges, tomatoes, carrots, potatoes, grapes), but they do not succeed in convincing the natives to adopt modern agricultural techniques nor to plant with a bit of planning. It is just as useless to try to teach them how to sew, to purify stagnant water, to apply the basic principles of hygiene. Respect for tradition is absolute, as is the rejection of anything new. The inhabitants despise the missionaries and do not understand their motivation for coming to the island.

Already exhausted by work and worry, these young missionaries are continually tormented by fevers and sickness, made worse by a lack of medicine and adequate nutrition. Mazzucconi is struck by malaria from the very beginning:

> In the first days of my stay on this island, the Lord sent me a fever; I have had it all year and still have it now… It begins with a chill throughout the body, and then the hands and fingernails become white and swollen; finally the cold becomes pervasive, you tremble all over and need to stay in bed. Here the confreres, as good as ever, cover you with whatever little we have, and there under the covers your teeth chatter constantly and you shiver for a few hours until the hot fever takes over; then your blood boils, it's as if your forehead is on fire, and if you've eaten anything it all comes up. Then sometimes there is delirium when you speak all the languages the Lord ever heard coming from earth. Then, after hours like this, so bad that you can hardly believe it, you say: Well, my Lord, this too has passed. You pick up your bed and take it out in the sun to dry and you have a good laugh with your confreres because your knees are still so weak, swollen, and painful that they can't support the weight of the covers much less that of the body, and you go tumbling to the ground.

Mazzucconi is in danger of death from these malarial fevers which strike him punctually each day at noon. His eyesight is also weakened from lack of food. "But in our house there was never any hunger; no, the main course was joy and contentment, which is really the greatest and richest gift that the Lord can give to His people on earth."

Fr. Reina writes on January 22, 1855:

> We are in a state of sickness and completely deprived of many things that are necessary for life; yet, there has never been a dark or discouraging day; you see in the hearts of my companions a tranquil peace, and in their behavior a light-hearted happiness.

And all of this, adds the missionary, despite the fact that precisely because of these continual fevers the natives despise them and believe them to be in the hands of an evil god.

To the physical suffering, then, is also added the feeling of failure. Yet John is able to write:

> To hear us speaking like this, one might be led to believe that we have done nothing for the mission this whole year. But I can tell you that we have done much, because we have suffered much, and I believe that this, united with our prayers, is the only way to call the mercy of God upon these people.

In January of 1855 the five missionaries find themselves in a disastrous situation. At least two (Catechist Corti and Mazzucconi himself) are almost at the end of their lives. Their bodies are swollen to incredible limits and the skin has begun to tear; they are covered with painful sores. Their teeth have turned black and the fever and delirium continue relentlessly. "Fr. Reina," John writes, "began to ask me certain questions — and I made out my will." He is not yet 29 years old.

With the three-month-late arrival of the hired ship two days before, the superior Reina orders Mazzucconi to leave the island and go to Australia to recuperate. But the captain of the ship, who needs to make numerous stops at commercial ports, is not sure that he wants to allow this "walking corpse" on board. He absolutely refuses to take on the catechist, who is unable to stand. During the journey he says to John: "Watching you come on board, I didn't believe that you could survive three months at sea, but now I am beginning to have hope." In fact, the maritime climate helps him to recover, so much so that the fever and the sores disappear.

In Sydney his health improves day by day and he looks forward to returning to his companions with fresh supplies.

On May 25 he wrote:

> This health is a gift from God, which must therefore be used for God. And that is what I will do. I will set out again on the first ship and return to the islands, see my "children" once again, embrace the confreres, and place myself anew in the service of God; then He will take care of the rest.

Thus, on August 18, 1855 he sails from Sydney on the little ship *Gazelle*. He doesn't know that Catechist Corti is dead and that notice has arrived from Rome that no other Italian missionary would be going there, lest more lives be put at risk. More than that, he has no idea that his companions, on evaluating their desperate situation, have decided to leave the islands at least temporarily, and are now on a voyage that has already lasted 40 days. They will arrive in Australia a few days after his departure.

In the first half of September the *Gazelle* enters the bay of Woodlark, and many natives gather on the beach. But the captain, unfamiliar with the waters, gets the ship caught up on the coral reef. From the shore comes a canoe with four men on board. Among them is Puarer, a friend of Fr. John, who informs him of the departure of his confreres. (Puarer would later recount the development of events.) Meanwhile, onshore, the natives decide to take advantage of the situation and release their pent-up hatred for the missionaries. They push off from shore in many canoes and surround the ship.

Two natives board the *Gazelle* and one of them, Aviocar, heads directly for the missionary with his hand extended as if in greeting. But then suddenly he pulls out an ax from beneath his loincloth and violently strikes at Fr. John's head. It is the beginning of the massacre. After John, all of the sailors are dismembered and their bodies are thrown into the sea.

A few months later, when Fr. Raimondi is finally able to return to Woodlark in search of his confrere, he finds only the upturned hull of the *Gazelle*, abandoned on the rocks.

A month before being killed, Fr. John had written from Sydney to his superior, Bishop Marinoni:

> I don't know what God has prepared for me on the journey which begins tomorrow. I only know one thing: that God is good and that He loves me immensely. All the rest, calm and storm, danger and security, life and death are nothing more than momentary and changing expressions of the eternal and unchanging Love.

On February 19, 1984, 129 years after his death, the martyr John Mazzucconi was proclaimed blessed by Pope John Paul II, in St. Peter's Basilica, Rome.

CHINA:
THE DRAGON VS.
THE "FOREIGN DEVILS"

CHINA

SHAANXI

Blessed
Alberic Crescitelli

SHAANXI

Xían

Hanzhong

Chenggu

Yanzibian

Guluba

Ningqiang

Han River

Shanghai

INTRODUCTION

By Fr. Giancarlo Politi, PIME

ALBERIC CRESCITELLI ARRIVED IN CHINA DURING ONE OF THE MOST important and tragic periods in the history of that country: the last years of the nineteenth century. The ruling regime, threatened by modernity and rotten to the core by the corruption of its officials, was on the way to an irreversible decline. The crisis of the reigning dynasty was but the most evident manifestation of the tragic ruin affecting the whole culture, which proved to be lacking the proper resources to encounter and interpret the challenges of a new world.

For centuries, the state functionary (the *mandarin*) had found his legitimacy and power in the classical texts; he was able to exercise his administrative duties through the rigid system of exams which were given annually at various levels. But these traditional texts were no longer able to offer adequate guidelines to confront the new demands of the country, such as the development of a modern highway system and a railway capable of fostering quick and efficient commerce.

Above all, these ancient texts completely ignored issues of vital importance, like the existence of other countries and cultures beyond the few surrounding ones, which were considered mere tributaries to the throne of the Son of Heaven. China, always proud of her own self-sufficiency and the fact that she had never needed any kind of equal relationship with the "barbarians" across the sea or beyond the great wall, was now finding herself incapable of preserving her precious isolation.

The nineteenth century, in fact, brought the Heavenly Empire into abrupt and sometimes brutal contact with the West. First to arrive were the commercial vessels, and then the warships of the European powers, with the mission to guard their interests. More and more arrived in succession, attracted by the fascination of this "new world" and the mirage of the commercial advantage that a "virgin" market presents. No one paid any attention to the indignant complaints of the regime, which felt threatened by these disrespectful savages who rejected any kind of proper etiquette.

In order to protect their trade, the foreign powers occupied the ports, substantial parts of the coastal territory, and blocks of the most important cities. Thus they established the *concessions*, zones which for all intents and purposes were controlled by foreigners.

The foreign navies brought their goods and supplies with them and, especially in the large cities, new products began to appear in great quantity and of better quality than had ever been seen before. Within a few years this caused a strong recession in the local economy, which lacked equal structures for creating work and trade.

Prices became disproportionate to the level of life not only of the common folks but also the middle class who worked for the state bureaucracy. Even the basic necessities gradually became too expensive for the people to buy. But the circle did not close at this point. Just as the goods became impossible for the Chinese to attain, the internal market was falling completely under foreign control and strangulation. The railroad revolutionized the system of communication, which for centuries had relied upon waterways, rivers, or imperial canals. The cities that had grown up along the water began to decline, while the new ones which sprang up along the railway lacked adequate infrastructure. As if all this were not enough, a series of natural calamities, like the flooding of the Yellow River, convinced the people, who were easily persuaded by those with their own self-interest, that the cause of all their troubles was the "foreign devils." Public opinion had it that they had damaged the veins of the dragon (a mythical animal which they believed to live under the earth) with the construction of the railroad and squandered his "precious breath" by systematically mining for minerals.

The intrusion of foreign powers provoked two reactions among members of the leading Chinese class, and thus two opposing movements. The conservatives wanted to do away with, or at least lessen, the threat imposed by contact with modernity. The reformers were aware of the seriousness of the situation and wanted to bring about a true transformation of the traditional, and now inadequate, mechanisms of government.

The reform movement was crushed during the coup of 1898, by the reactionary Manchu group, which took complete power and eliminated any radical or moderate faction favoring socio-political reform in China. On the Grand Council of the Empire were Jung Lu, Yu Lu and Ch'i Siu, while General Secretary Kang Yi, conservative to the extreme, gained ever greater influence over the Empress Cixi. Unable to understand the complexity of international politics and the gravity of the moment, these men rejected in principle any kind of diplomacy or compromise, insisting instead upon a policy of strict resistance. The empress, under their influence, ordered that no more concessions be made to the foreign powers. This extreme and vain decree stands out for its total lack of realism.

The reform movement having been eliminated, the leaders, and gradually also the intellectual class, the nobility, and the people in general, became convinced that China's troubles had only one origin: foreign intrusion. A deep sense of xenophobia ensued, resulting in aversion for anything foreign, while at the same time a strong protectionist movement began to develop. The previous fifty years of continual humiliation had a profound effect upon the national consciousness, bringing about a burning desire for revenge.

In April of 1898, those in the capital began to fear that China would be colonized in the same way as Burma, Annam (the central part of present day Vietnam) and India. The central government was dominated by incompetent ministers and a meddlesome regent, Empress Cixi. If before they had been merely fumbling, now they were leading China to the end of the century in total paralysis. To prolong the survival of the regime, Cixi, a master of intrigue, came up with an idea that only she could conceive: she hired ancient enemies of the throne in order to use them for her own purposes.

The *Boxers* (Yihetuan, meaning harmony and justice) were a secret society which came into being a century before in the province of Shandong. Between 1896 and 1904, they conducted a revolutionary movement against the Qing dynasty, a rebellion which quickly spread to the neighboring provinces of Henan and Kiangnan (currently Anhui and Jiansu). The sect continued to exist even after the suppression of the revolt. Fifteen years later, they changed their course and began to control gambling in the cities, and to operate a protection racket. The business initiatives of the foreigners were damaging the interests of the Boxers as well, and by 1890 these organized crime bosses began to see every foreigner as a dangerous competitor to be eliminated. The politicians of Shandong seized the opportunity to reinforce anti-foreigner feelings in the leaders of the sect.

The recruiting of members was carried out among the least desirable of people, those referred to in street language as *tu fei* (the bandits). They were initiated in complex rituals which included the teaching of magic and the use of amulets and incantations to make them invulnerable to bullets.

It was actually the governor of Shandong who suggested that the Imperial Court use this sect to resolve the problem of the "hairy people," as the foreigners came to be called. The Court eagerly agreed: the Boxers would defend the throne against the invaders, who must be completely destroyed. The enemy was classified into three categories of people: all foreigners on national land, Chinese Christians, and merchants who dealt with foreigners. Later, those who used foreign products would also be included. These types of people were condemned to extermination. Missionaries were allotted the same fate.

The Tianjin treaties of 1858, imposed with force by the West, had permitted missionaries to spread Christianity throughout the country. Two years later, in 1860, the Conventions of Peking granted missionaries the right to rent or buy property for the construction of churches and other works. These were decisive changes from previous periods.

The most relevant consequence of these treaties was that missionaries were able to move about freely through the country, protected by the respective consular authorities. The work of the missionaries in this period has often been criticized harshly. In fact, though, no serious, systematic study has been done to give a global analysis of the missionary efforts carried out in China during these decades. It would be unfair to make unqualified and rash judgments, using generalizations, partial truths, and diverse opinions which have not been critically analyzed. Many of these missionaries were men honestly filled with the love of God, conscious of their limitations and sometimes also critical of the methods used to make the church visible in this immense country. This having been said, it must be admitted that there were few conversions, and more than a few missionaries resorted to questionable practices in order to secure a decent number of baptisms. For once, the Chinese bourgeois and nobility agreed with the intellectuals in considering Christianity socially negative, delusional, and something of a heretical sect.

Within a few months, among the Catholics, five bishops, dozens of missionary priests and religious, and more than thirty thousand Chinese Christians were killed. The blood bath was interrupted only through the armed intervention of the foreign powers. Though they resented the intervention, they nevertheless desisted without admitting any responsibility.

BLESSED ALBERIC CRESCITELLI

(JUNE 30, 1863 – JULY 21, 1900)

It is August 17, 1888, and another interminable day is finally coming to an end. For the oarsmen the day has been tiring, and no less so for Fr. Alberic Crescitelli and his confrere, Fr. Vincenzo Colli. Since March 30 the boat has been slowly making its way along the Han River from the port of Hankou to Xiaozhai, the final destination of the two missionaries.

Fr. Alberic has already retired to the tiny sleeping quarters of the passengers, a small hut with a woven roof and walls made of branches, so badly constructed that wind and rain, and stench and smoke from the nearby kitchen enter freely.

From the stern come the subdued voices of the Chinese oarsmen who, tired after the long day, smoke tobacco or opium while playing cards. Rolled up in a dirty blanket next to Fr. Vincenzo, who in the Chinese custom is lying with his feet next to the other's face, Fr. Crescitelli is exhausted. After 132 days at sea from Marseilles to Shanghai, this endless journey lies ahead. Just how much further is the mission? He cannot sleep. He thinks about the effort put forth by these Chinese workers. "The Lord helped us again today. We did not meet with misfortune. Yet I wonder how the boat was able to withstand ramming so many rocks. At some points the current was so strong that 50 men had to struggle to keep a steady course." It has been some time since they left the monotonous landscape of the vast lowlands, interrupted only by rare willow trees and small, miserable houses. All the oarsmen needed to do then was haul the boat along with bamboo ropes, rhythmically walking along one side or the other of the river.

Then the hills gave way to precipitous mountains and the course of the river became more and more impenetrable. The pullers had to use superhuman effort to overcome the current and the helmsman needed the greatest care and ability to prevent the hull from smashing against the rocks which suddenly appeared in the foaming water.

Today, more than once in the more dangerous places, the passengers have to get off the boat and walk along the river bank . "Oh, surely I would not have the courage to follow this river to the end, I'm sure I would be tempted to give up everything if I were not sustained by such a great goal," Fr. Alberic confesses.

He allows his mind to drift. For a moment he is able to forget the discomforts of the journey, as in his mind he runs among the green hills of Southern Italy where he spent so much time working the fields of his father. In fact, while he was still a boy, just finished with elementary school, his father, the pharmacist of Altavilla, decided that out of his ten sons, Alberic would be the one to oversee the work in the fields. He was the strongest and brightest.

For years he willingly dedicated himself to this work, but in 1878, at the age of 15, he decided to resume his studies. He had already been using some of his free time to escape to the library of Fr. Raffaele Crescitelli, to soak up stories of history, spirituality, and liturgy, until reading had become his favorite hobby.

He also remembers, as if it were yesterday, the departure of his brother Luigi for military service. Alberic had been declared physically unfit and he talked to his mother about this "privilege." One discussion led to another and finally he had the courage to confide to her a desire he had been cultivating for two years: to become a missionary.

His memories pass to his seminary years. He remembers that distant November 8, 1880, when he entered the Pontifical Seminary of Sts. Peter and Paul in Rome,[1] the hard work and passion with which he

---

[1] A missionary institute of secular priests founded in Rome, at the direction of Pope Pius IX, by Bishop Pietro Avanzini in 1871, with the identical characteristics as the Seminary for Foreign Missions in Milan (e.g. direct dependence upon the Sacred Congregation for the Propagation of the Faith). In view of their similarities, in 1912

studied Latin, philosophy, and theology, interspersed with the joy of vacations in his home village. But he also cannot forget the sad summer of 1883, when his father and his sister Rosina were buried beneath the rubble of Casamicciola during a violent earthquake; nor the cholera epidemic which broke out in Campania in 1887, right after his priestly ordination. Already assigned to China and home for a final vacation, he had to delay his departure. For four long and exhausting months, he dedicated himself to assisting the cholera victims of his village. And once more his memories are invaded by the image of death which he witnessed in the faces of so many friends.

The cries of the Chinese draw him back from his melancholy reverie. The pigtail of his confrere tickles his feet. To become Chinese with the Chinese, the two missionaries adopted the local style of dress, and so, placed themselves under the scissors of a barber and in the care of a tailor as soon as they landed. Fr. Alberic laughs at himself. He has had problems with baldness since his youth; now at the age of 25 he has hardly any hair at all. He tried to grow the complex braid down the middle of his neck, but it is short and silly looking. To make up for it he must wear a cap with a false pigtail attached. And then there is the shirt that reaches all the way to his feet, with its extra wide sleeves. He thinks about the photo he sent to his brother Luigi: "I know I'm almost unrecognizable, dressed this way, but it's really me!"

Cradled in these thoughts, he finally falls asleep. This time, however, when he awakens, there are Italian voices mixed in with the cries of the crowd gathered on the river bank.

It is August 18, 1888. The sun is already high in the sky. Finally, after 81 days on the Han River, Frs. Crescitelli and Colli have arrived at Xiaozhai, a town of ancient Christianity. His confreres, who have been stationed here for three years, are waiting for them.

They have 10 days of rest after the exhausting journey, and then the two missionaries move on to Hanzhong, seat of the Apostolic Vic-

---

the two institutes requested to be unified. Thus, in 1926, with the approval of Pius XI, the Pontifical Institute for Foreign Missions (P.I.M.E.) was born, with headquarters in Milan.

ariate of southern Shaanxi, in order to undergo the "intellectual torture of studying the Chinese language."

After only nine months of study, Fr. Alberic is assigned the district of Sijiaying which extends among the hills and valleys surrounding the Han River: a thousand Christians in seven villages.

Very active in the care of the Christians and in the formation of catechumens, he ventures far and wide in the territory assigned to him. He travels through the dangerous mountains and the muddy lowlands, all covered with rice paddies. Walking is difficult for him because of a congenital illness; and so while stumbling along the nearly impenetrable trails, he is forced, much to his disgust, to be carried on a litter. The frequent travels oblige him to accept lodging wherever he can, even among the pagans, because the Christians who live in the mountains are very poor. A straw hut, smoky quarters, some damp and dark corner, a cold and dirty floor: these are his accommodations. He tries to sleep and celebrate Mass everywhere: "Any place where you can bless and console a soul, where the people are poorest, where there is much pain and suffering … is a place of honor for a minister of the church." Fr. Alberic always maintains a peaceful tranquillity: "My heart tells me that I am where I belong, where God wants me, and I am happy."

But while his spirit of adaptation is truly admirable, he is tormented by another kind of suffering. Among the trials he endures, perhaps the most difficult is the apparent ineffectiveness of his efforts. "The Chinese remain indifferent, if not directly hostile." Still, he writes to his brother:

> Who is happy here on earth? You often believe that you're unhappy, but there are many people more unhappy than you! I'm also a man subject to sufferings. I have moments of boredom, of struggle, of disillusion, of temptation, of unknown danger and trial. Who on earth can escape from these? Yet, up to now, I believe that I have been happier than most people. In whatever country we live, Providence gives us strength proportionate to our sufferings so that we might bear them

worthily, and it is even better when we are where God wants us to be. Actually, I'm doing quite well.

And so he continues, catechizing, defending the weak by aiding them when they are in need, teaching agriculture, and buying little plots of land so the poor and homeless have the basics to live. Nevertheless, he is not always accepted with enthusiasm, nor even respect. Indeed, his optimism is quite bewildering, since throughout the whole of China there is a thinly veiled form of persecution against Christians and foreign missionaries, who are considered to be tied in with the foreign powers and complicit in their policy of penetrating the Heavenly Empire.

Alarming news of disorder and persecution has reached Italy, but Fr. Alberic writes to his worried mother: "Why are you afraid? We are in the hands of God… Therefore we do His will and that's enough… As long as the Lord gives me the strength, anything that happens to me will be for my good." And again:

> Don't worry about me; if you've heard that in other provinces of China, butchery has occurred, you should be persuaded by my previous letters that there is nothing to fear here, unless something completely unforeseen should happen. The Christians here, unlike in other areas, are united, and the non-Christians fear and respect us, so they do not dare to do us any harm. Besides, the nature of the people is peaceful and in general the Christians and non-Christians live together in peace. As far as the mandarins are concerned, as much as they might wish evil upon us, they must know that even if they have secret orders to obstruct our work, the Imperial Court certainly would not want an outright persecution, which would embarrass the government. They are only interested in maintaining order, and since the Christians are numerous and united, it would be dangerous for the mandarins to move against them without risking losing their position. You only need to

notice that even during the fiercest persecutions, the mandarins of this area were moderate in carrying out the imperial decrees. There have never been any real massacres of Christians here in Shangyuanguan. I know of only one Chinese priest who died a martyr at the hands of the mandarin when the persecution was raging. During that same time many were beaten and exiled, but no one was ever tortured.

Meanwhile, however, the reform movement having been crushed in 1898, the anti-foreign battle begins to explode openly and involves more and more secret nationalist societies. One of the societies is the Boxers, at first quietly supported and sustained by some functionaries of the government, and finally openly encouraged by the empress herself. As these two forces joined together, the massacres and attacks spread quickly, especially in Shaanxi, where in 1898 a new governor is installed: Yu Xian, bitter enemy of foreigners and protector of the Boxers. They create training centers, destroy railroad tracks and knock down telegraph poles. An especially furious attack is directed at the Christians. They are despised and denigrated, losing more and more of their social and human rights.

It is in this context that Fr. Alberic is transferred to a new district, Ningqiang, in 1900. It is a wild place, among high mountains furrowed by rivers and deep valleys, and peopled by the descendants of forced labor convicts and those exiled for criminal activities. It is a place, then, far from the influence of the government and difficult to reach, a place which favors the development of secret societies, hostile to any type of legal authority. Besides all of this, the area in which Fr. Crescitelli arrives is suffering from a terrible famine.

Fr. Alberic knows very well the situation he will face, but he is ready for anything:

> Who knows how it will go in this distant district. At any rate, life and death are both in the hands of God: not a leaf drops that God does not will... Be of good cheer and don't worry about me. I am in the hands of

God and I'm happy. My guardian angel is watching over
me... I expect enormous work awaiting me, which is
much better than the boredom of idleness!

And so he sets off once more into unknown territory. During the
journey he comes into contact right away with the sad reality he has
heard about. Along the road is a succession of ruins: tumble-down
houses whose roofs have been removed to sell the tiles; filthy hovels
from which emerge emaciated children with clouded and haunted
eyes. Women, like walking corpses, are going through the refuse, looking for something to sell or to eat. There is nothing edible, and many
are reduced to gathering the bark of trees, which they will cook together with roots of grass to make some kind of meal. According to imperial law, public granaries should provide for the people in time of
famine, but these have already been ransacked by the civilian militias.
Grain is still abundant in nearby provinces, but no one bothers to send
it. Fortunately the local authorities, who have appealed to Peking for
the suspension of taxes and for food aid, succeed in having the imperial
army bring rice into the area.

But absolutely no help is given to the Christians. According to
Teng, a pumped up braggart who plays boss in the area, who has
grown rich through extortion and is hostile to Christians, they are trai-
tors to China; in fact, they are no longer even Chinese, but "foreign
devils" who follow Western doctrines. Thus, they can no longer claim
any rights in Chinese society. Fr. Crescitelli opposes these abuses with
all his power. He appeals to the mandarin of the city, who admits that
he is right; but this only increases the hatred toward the foreigner
among the leading men, who desire revenge.

The situation is becoming more and more critical, as vague and
anxious rumors begin to circulate. His death is being planned. But Fr.
Alberic seems not to notice. Rather, satisfied that he has obtained some
food for the Christians, even though they are given half rations and it
is wheat rather than rice, he writes to the Apostolic Vicar on July 10,
1900: "In Yanzibian peace reigns like never before and the quarrel has
ended as if by magic." It is the calm before the storm.

While all of this is happening, an imperial decree comes from Peking, sentencing to death all Christians who do not renounce their religion and ordering the deportation of all foreign missionaries. The viceroy of Shaanxi does not publish the decree, but the enemies of Fr. Alberic find out about it, and fearing that they will not be able to do away with the missionary legally, begin to plot with the mandarin of Ningqiang to kill him.

The catechumens, however, become aware of the danger and hurry to warn him so that he can flee far from the district. But Fr. Alberic believes it would be unworthy and unjust to abandon his Christians at the very moment of their greatest danger, and he stops in Tsinkangping, only about half a kilometer from Yanzibian. On July 20 the territorial guard sack the house of the catechist, and Fr. Alberic, aware that his presence might cause more violence, decides with a heavy heart to leave the mission and place himself under the protection of the mandarin's authority. Sad and embittered, he gathers up his meager belongings in two baskets and rides on horseback toward the countryside, accompanied by his catechists and a few Christians.

But it's too late. Night is falling, and suddenly the customs official Jao che appears. He insists that Father spend the night with him because, he says, the streets are not safe, but in the customs house there is nothing to fear. The missionary finally accepts. Later, however, beset by sad foreboding and moved by the insistent pleas of his friends, he senses the trap and attempts to continue his journey: "There are a hundred armed men out looking for you; this is the only safe place," reiterates the customs official, convincing him once and for all to stay.

In the deep silence of the night, three mortar rounds are fired. This is the signal. Many people gather at the door of the customs house demanding to take the "European devil." The customs official, pretending sorrow, says to the missionary: "You see how many people are gathered against you. It's impossible for me to defend you. The only means of escape, if you can make it, is the back door, which faces the mountain." And he pushes him out of the house. But escape to where? The wall of the mountain, pressing in close on the house, is impenetrable. Fr. Alberic knows that there is no escape. He kneels and prays.

By now the tumultuous crowd is surrounding him. "Why are you doing this?" Fr. Alberic asks his attackers. "What have I done to you? If you have something against me, some accusation to make, speak; take me to the authorities." The only response is a fierce blow to his left arm, almost severing it, and then another directly to his face, breaking open his nose and his lips. Dazed by the blows of the clubs and by his wounds, he is at first dragged, and then because of his large body, they force a catechumen to carry him on his shoulders. Finally, after tying his hands and feet to a pole, they carry him like an animal on the way to the butcher.

Thrown down in the marketplace of Yanzibian, Fr. Alberic remains the target of the fierce crowd, which continues to inflict countless tortures upon him. Thus he passes the night, alternating between moments of delirium and clarity, during which he prays for his attackers, who pass the time by getting drunk and playing cards.

Morning comes and the sun is already high in the sky when the assassins finally decide to finish the job. But while they are discussing how to kill the missionary, a military mandarin arrives, having been informed of the proceedings by catechists the night before. He has twenty soldiers with him, but he quickly realizes that in the face of this crowd, they will not be able to restore order nor to help the Father. He exhorts the people not to kill him and then goes in search of some means to get him to a doctor. But while the captain and his soldiers are looking for a stretcher, Fr. Alberic is dragged by a rope to the bank of the river which flows near the marketplace and there he is decapitated, his body dismembered and cast into the river.

It is just past noon on July 21, 1900. Fr. Alberic Crescitelli is 37 years old. Like him, thousands of Christians are killed during the Boxer rebellion in China.

On February 18, 1951, Pope Pius XII declared him blessed.

CHINA, 1941:
ACTORS IN A
THEATER OF WAR

Fr. Cesare Mencattini

Bishop Antonio Barosi

Fr. Mario Zanardi

Fr. Bruno Zanella

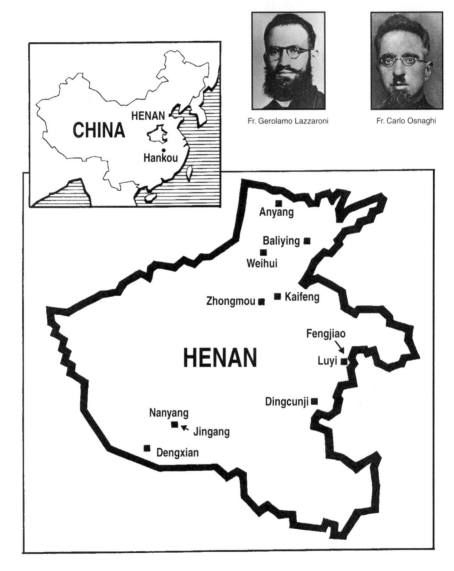

Fr. Gerolamo Lazzaroni

Fr. Carlo Osnaghi

CHINA

HENAN

Hankou

HENAN

Anyang

Baliying ■

Weihui

Zhongmou ■ ■ Kaifeng

Fengjiao

Luyi ■

Dingcunji ■

Nanyang

■ Jingang

■ Dengxian

INTRODUCTION

By Fr. Giancarlo Politi, PIME

DURING THE LONG SINO-JAPANESE WAR (1937–45), CHINA WAS A blood bath. Fr. Cesare Mencattini; the group of Bishop Antonio Barosi, Frs. Mario Zanardi, Bruno Zanella and Gerolamo Lazzaroni; and finally Fr. Carlo Osnaghi, were all killed in the province of Henan during that time.

Japan began promoting Manchurian-Mongolian movements for independence as part of its plan of aggression against China the day after having annexed Korea in 1910. This was in keeping with the logic of the militarists of the Japanese empire, that "to conquer the world, we must first conquer China; and to conquer China, we must first conquer Manchuria and Mongolia." The events of 1941 were the culmination of plans which had been brewing for a long time.

The site of the killings was Henan province, strategically located in the middle of the most important provinces of the time: Hebei to the north, Shaanxi to the west, Hubei to the south, and Anhui and Jiangsu to the east. Poor and lacking in industry (agriculture had always been its only resource), the immense plain of Henan was fertile, but often covered by the flood waters of the mighty Yellow River. It had been the battle ground for many armies attempting to gain control of the surrounding provinces.

The Sino-Japanese war was followed by four more years of civil war (1945-49) between the nationalists and the communists. The well-known result was the victory of the latter, and the installation of a new, revolutionary government in Peking, which was immediately pro-claimed the capital. Yet, not even the preceding decades had been peaceful, since the country had become nothing more than a war theater among the many groups who wanted to obtain political dominance.

The long period of hostilities and the absence of any effective central authority permitted the rise of many armies and armed bands, each one dedicated to asserting its own authority by force and violence. Besides the nationalist and the red armies, several armed bands were relatively well organized and controlled slices of territory, even whole provinces.

Similar conditions and motivations moved the soldiers of these armies: if they were paid at all, it was only occasionally and inadequately; so one of their first concerns was food and maybe something more (gold, money, and valuables for example). They also shared a hatred for foreigners, fueled by the ever growing xenophobic campaign. Indeed, most of the factions in China were able to benefit by attributing all of the country's ills to foreigners.

The soldiers of the red army also took part in actions of reprisals, thefts, and lootings. It has only been the propaganda of the victorious military regime which has sought to make them appear to have been altruistic and absolutely respectful of persons and property. The reality was quite different. The red bands were guilty of innumerable atrocities against humanity. Unlike other armed groups, they had a specific anti-religious objective which they carried out to infamous extremes. Just among the Catholics, one can count many, many priests, religious, and faithful who were killed, often in the most barbarous way, in the areas under communist control before the proclamation of the People's Republic.

During the years of the Sino-Japanese war, robberies and killings continued among Chinese belonging to different factions and political leanings; and now a new player entered the fray: the occupying Japanese army. Who committed the most crimes and massacres is anybody's guess.

These political convulsions brought an endless series of killings, suffering, and brutality to the Chinese people. Christians and missionaries, that is, both Chinese and foreigners, shared the same fate: Christians at the hands of their own and the missionaries at the hands of those they had come to serve. They both were victims of a world view dominated by the party interests and ideologies of a particular time and place.

FR. CESARE MENCATTINI

(MAY 7, 1910 – JULY 12, 1941)

September 17, 1927: the doorbell of the P.I.M.E. seminary at Agazzi, in the Arezzo province, rings loud and long. Looking out of the window, the rector sees a young man standing in front of the door, with sparkling eyes and a determined face: "Will you take me? I want to be a missionary!"

He is from Bibbiena; he is seventeen years old and his name is Cesare Mencattini. It has been five years since he left home to attend, first the seminary of Arezzo, and then, due to delicate health, that of Cortona, where he completed his high-school studies with honors.

Now, however, the desire to be a good diocesan priest is not enough for him. The idea of the missions has been constantly growing in him, so much so that one thought has almost become a personal slogan: "So many poor without Christ are waiting to hear the message of God."

The road ahead is still long, but his enthusiasm never wavers.

He likes to study and does so with dedication, but whenever he can he spends some days in the nearby forest of Camaldoli, immersed in silence and in nature which enchants and uplifts him, reinvigorating him after months of being cooped up with his books.

His spirit is enraptured by the marvels of creation. During one trip, after a night spent with his friends counting the stars, he sees the top of Mount Pratomagno, on which a gigantic cross is mounted. "That site," he would write years later, "inspired in us a great desire to conquer that proud mountaintop. We walked the paths of the mountain chain which separates Valdarno from Casentino. A little before nine o'clock we crossed the beautiful grasslands that were like a velvet carpet... Oh, the wonderful sights of that valley!"

His spirit is lifted up to God as he climbs Mt. Verna:

> We passed through Abetone and by the rock of Frate Lupo; from the terrace of the Penna we could never tire of admiring that enchanted Valle Santa! I could have stayed there for hours in meditation... The vast horizons invite the soul to grow, they inspire great things, and we felt on top of the world... There, from that mountaintop, St. Francis could very well have sung the Canticle of the Creatures...

Upon finishing theology studies at the P.I.M.E. seminary in Monza, he prepares for the priesthood: "Let's not think that we can take any credit before God by becoming missionaries! We are always debtors to the Lord for this great grace which we will never understand while we are in this world." In Christmas greetings to his younger brother Pasquale, a seminarian in Cortona, he writes:

> Soon we will be priests, in keeping with the mystery of the feast we're celebrating now! Our priestly life will be a continual hymn of "Glory to God" and a constant message of "Peace to men..." As much as you can imagine the sacrifices of our vocation, you will never be able to fully understand them. We have to be ready for anything...

His greatest ambition is to put into practice the example of Christ, but he is also aware of his own weakness and understands that to be prepared to take on such suffering, he needs to be well trained; and his "training" even includes undergoing a surgical operation, without anesthesia.

On September 22, 1934 Cesare is ordained a priest.

During his brief stay with his family, he is already acting like a missionary, preaching retreats, visiting the sick in the hospital, and attending missionary meetings in Casentino.

On August 9, 1935, at the appropriate hour of sunset, in the faint light of the Institute's chapel, the Superior General greets the new missionaries with the words of Jesus to His apostles: "I'm sending you like sheep among wolves..." and speaks of the difficulty of their choice without hiding his fears and hopes.

Twelve years of formation, a vocation nurtured for so long a time, and now they were close to realizing their dream. "I have a feeling," writes Fr. Cesare, "that I will go to China, because that's where most of the assignments are destined this year. And this is really where I want to go, because it is currently the place where there is the greatest hope to crown our lives with the tiara of martyrdom." This thought accompanies Cesare and his companions as, from the train windows, they watch the figures of their families and friends at the Milan station recede in the distance. At that time, departures were characterized by a knot in the throat and a look in the eyes that said: We'll never see you again, except in heaven.

After a long sea voyage, Fr. Cesare arrives in Shanghai on September 10, 1935:

> I am so happy to arrive and to be able to give God this proof that I love Him, leaving behind the persons and things held most dear... I am in my adopted country. I thank the Lord that He has brought me here among the Chinese. Now I must acclimate myself and die to my own way of living, in order to adopt a new one.

It's not easy. During the nine months of language study at the P.I.M.E. Regional House in Kaifeng, he can already recognize the difficulties a missionary must confront:

> Immense populations live here in desolation and misery in regions which extend for hundreds of kilometers. We missionaries could not reach everyone, even if we had wings. We're limited to doing very little in comparison with the immense work there is to accomplish. The inhabitants of these areas are reduced to the most

extreme poverty, the results of brigands' passing, war, and the flooding of the Yellow River. Along the roads you see groups of vagabonds, who don't even have a hole in which to spend the night nor sufficient clothes to guard against the cold, which is so intense here in Henan.

You can't imagine what it's like for us missionaries to live here. Not only are there the physical sufferings, which are very real, but we also have the feeling of being alone in the midst of these people who regard us with indifference and disdain. We're often the object of insulting words. When they see us walking by, for example, they say, "Here comes a European dog." If only they knew how much good we wish them and the sacrifices we have made and are making in order to live in their midst!

But Fr. Mencattini is not discouraged, because he knows that he remains in the hands of God, even in this "desert of yellow sand, so small and fine that you find it settling in your eyes, your ears, everywhere... In this unlimited lowland, where everything looks the same... What a contrast to the enchanting green vistas of Casentino!"

Still, he is able to be happy. In fact, in June of 1936, when he is sent to the vast district of Huaxian as assistant to Fr. Paolo Giusti, he writes to his brother:

I am happy to be a gypsy priest, without a church, without a rectory, without benefits, but rich in souls, lacking in clout but renewed by grace! My Christians are poor but truly good! They are so attentive when I speak of the goodness of God and eternal life! Then they all kneel on the bare earth, under the stars, to pray... Tell me, if this is not true happiness! After having lived for six days in ratholes with beds of mud, this room of mine is worth more to me than the salon of His Majesty the King of Italy and the Emperor of

Ethiopia. I assure you that I am truly happy, because I have a contented heart: content that I have left my loved ones in order to turn all of my affections toward God and toward the many poor people who are so dear to me now that they have been reborn in baptism; content that I traded the beauty of Italy for this desert of yellow sand which is becoming as familiar to me as my own village; content that I left behind my studies, to which I dedicated such effort, to become ignorant and to express the beauty of our religion in a language which is not my own, using only the most elementary terms and simplest comparisons; content to do without the grand liturgies of our Catholic countries in order to celebrate the Mass and administer the sacraments in rustic and poor chapels...

Thus Fr. Cesare throws himself into the "excursions" through the endless plains of the Yellow River.

Leaving his "headquarters" at Baliying every Monday morning, he goes by bicycle to visit the Christian villages, returning home each Saturday evening for Sunday Mass.

My work consists not so much in increasing the number of Christians as in reorganizing the communities, making sure that each one has a mud chapel or at least a roof of straw under which to gather for prayer, training catechists to lead the people, establishing a fund in each village to cover the inevitable expenses...

Just as Fr. Cesare is beginning to see the first promising results of his pastoral plan, the Sino-Japanese war breaks out, and the future becomes increasingly dark. He has to suspend his plan to open schools, send the catechists home, and confront the most urgent needs of the people.

In 1937 the Japanese advance becomes ever more alarming: trenches and suspicions begin to appear.

The hostilities begin. By January of 1938 the war is raging, and in between brief periods of truce, there are fierce bombings: "All of the authorities have disappeared. With the continual passage of soldiers, the food supply, already diminished by the damage done to the harvest by the floods, is almost gone. Looting and famine are inevitable."

Fr. Cesare often moves up to the front lines to assist the wounded, comfort the dying, and bury the dead. He is often chased and captured by the troops of one party or another. Finally, in February of 1939, the Japanese establish a garrison in Huaxian to control the city and ransack the countryside.

> The Chinese, so lacking in arms and unable to resist the Japanese, who advance with cannons and automobiles, have adopted this defensive tactic: they destroy all the roads... Thousands of people have been commandeered for this immense work; night and day for two months, they have dug deep pits in all the streets. The painful effort, which the people must put forth with no compensation, is more than you can imagine. There is the added danger of being surprised by the Japanese. Even my bicycle paths have become difficult. On my last trip I had to pedal through the fields and cross from one pit to another with my bike on my back.
>
> They hope to make it impossible for the autos and armed carriers of the Japanese to pass through. Instead, the Japanese, even with ten cars and several large cannons, have easily reached this area and surrounded it.
>
> The current conditions for us missionaries are difficult. The Japanese have a garrison in the city; but outside, on the pretext of defending the country, great numbers of soldiers roam about, harassing the poor people so much that they are called "soldiers who eat everything." We are in the middle. We are doomed if we do not remain neutral! It would be impossible for us to stay.

The places once occupied by the Japanese and often abandoned because of their poor condition, fall into the hands of the communists or other soldiers, or brigands. The city of Huaxian has suffered this fate five times in one year: occupied by regular troops, the Japanese, brigands, the communists, and now once again the Japanese, who are quickly working to rebuild it.

What ruin! The destruction caused by passing soldiers is worse than that caused by cannons or bombs dropped from airplanes. After a voluntary retreat of the Japanese, when the Chinese take over the city again, everything is destroyed. Railway stations, city walls, everything must be reduced to heaps of rubble.

For more than a year there has been no commerce, no schools, no authority — only disorder and confusion which seem to have no end in sight.

The war seems like it will go on forever.

At the beginning of 1941, describing the chaotic situation in which he still finds himself, Fr. Cesare writes:

I've been wanting to write to you for some time, but the conditions here have prevented me. I wish I could describe to you the world in which we live! You would wonder how it is that no missionary has been killed so far in Weihui. I will try to tell you something. For four years I have been in charge of the same district, and I have not had one day of peace. The war is always here.

My entire area has been and is always full of soldiers, who cause quite a few troubles for us. What a strange war! The front is everywhere. It's impossible to understand anything amid this disorder. I can't find the words to give you an idea of it. There are the communists. They work through fear, always moving about and operating in the night. It will be bad for us if they are able to establish themselves here. I have met up with them four or five times. Truly, I was only saved by the protection of the Lord. The first time, they fired three shots at me, but were not able to hit me, nor the servant with me, although the bullets whizzed by our heads and backs. The second time they took away my chalice and pyx, and tore up my missal. A third time, at night while I was returning from giving last rites, they stopped me at rifle point. A few days ago they tried to take me with them, but they soon released me, without even searching me. Luckily, they cannot stay in one place very long. They are constantly under the attack of the Japanese and the soldiers of the old government. Then there are also the soldiers of the new government.

You can add, finally, a multitude of brigands, who try to bite off more than they can chew, committing all sorts of crimes and robberies. Among their victims are two catechists who were taken away: one was buried alive and the other was decapitated.

Imagine the confusion with all the different types of guerrillas! I am always in the middle. It's been going on for more than three and a half years, and who knows when it will end?

One day we're under one group, the next day another. Always thinking of the best way to get along with all of them, I try to continue my work. As you can see, I'm in a difficult and dangerous position. In these past months, almost every day you can see villages in flames, while rifle volleys are heard almost constantly. And we stay here, waiting for it to pass.

Just now as I am writing this, not far away I can hear gunshots, and the crackle of machine-gun fire. Maybe it is the brigands attacking a village; maybe it is the communists battling with the soldiers of the new government.

As soon as night falls, I can be sure to hear the rumble of the cannon, with which the Japanese, for the moment, are routing these scraggly soldiers.

In spite of such chaos, I have been able to build a small chapel. It is a luxury in these parts, where there is not a more beautiful structure. The walls are made of mud, covered by bricks on the outside. I have in mind to decorate the unadorned walls and to build a decent altar to replace the wobbly table we now use.

I also want to build a dryer, healthier house for myself. The wood is ready. Then the hall for teaching catechumens, the school ... What dreams!

If only the war would end! That is my dream, my greatest hope. I'm so tired of this chaotic life, and so sick of seeing such misery and broken bodies. I don't know how much more I can take, feeling the tears and groans of so many.

In our vicariate, many missionaries are failing in health. But I can still be counted among the healthy ones.

Even though he knows that the situation is getting more and more dangerous and could explode at any moment, Fr. Mencattini decides to stay at his post. Indeed, back in July of 1939 he has written: "Many times I get on my knees expecting to die. But I have never left my post. If I have to lose my life for the sake of my ministry, I will be truly happy."

In 1940 they decide to stay on as well even though cholera strikes. The workload is great; Fr. Cesare comes down with virulent dysentery; Fr. Giusti has malaria. And even the bishop calls them back. Still they stay on.

The opportunities for doing good are so great here! Many of the poor have no one else to help them... We have no fear of death here. We would really be leaving nothing behind in this poor world. All of our strength, energy and health must be dedicated to the Chinese, until we can do no more.

They have to go to the farthest reaches of the district to console the people, help hundreds and hundreds of refugees and sick, bury the dead. The bishop is forced to give in to their determination.

Then, suddenly, a telegram arrives in Italy, addressed to the Superior General of P.I.M.E.: "On July 12, 1941, Fr. Cesare Mencattini fell victim to an assault by a straggling band of Chinese soldiers. In the same incident Frs. Angelo Bagnoli and Leo Cavallini were wounded." The telegram gives no details, and the superior must wait until November to find out the particulars. The facts are finally reconstructed in a letter from Fr. Sordo, the procurator in the Hong Kong mission.

On the evening of July 11, after an exhausting journey on bicycle under the searing sun, Fr. Cesare arrives in Huaxian from Baliying. He has come to meet Fr. Giusti and the two of them plan to negotiate the purchase of some land in order to build a school for girls. They decide to speak to the bishop. The next day, Fr. Cesare plans to go to Weihui in the company of Frs. Bagnoli and Cavallini.

Thus, after the dawn celebration of the Mass on July 12, the three depart. Fr. Cesare is on his bicycle, being towed by the motorcycle ridden by the other two. Around nine o'clock the small band reaches the market of Qimen. Everything seems quiet; no one could foresee that at the same time some irregular soldiers, said to be connected with the mandarin of Rencun, would arrive. The fathers, just a few hundred meters from the entrance of the market are shot without warning by these soldiers, who have hidden themselves behind a small wall surrounding the market. All three are hit by the dum-dum bullets. Fr. Mencattini falls to the ground with a painful cry, his stomach ripped open by the bullets. They finish him off immediately with a bayonet and after stealing everything, including his clothes, they bury him.

Fr. Bagnoli, wounded in the left leg, has just enough time to call out his name and give him absolution. Fr. Cavallini, hit in the left foot, has a fractured ankle and falls with the motorcycle into a ditch on the side of the road. Fr. Bagnoli tries desperately to stop the brigands, explaining that they are Catholic missionaries, but they only reply, "We know." Then they get a cart and carry the two wounded fathers into the market. They put them under a pagoda where they remain until four o'clock in the afternoon. Anyone who tries to come close or to help them is threatened.

The two survivors are condemned to be buried alive, but providentially an influential Christian official who has heard of the events arrives on the scene. After hours of discussion he is able to free them from the hands of their assailants. Then, in two barrows pushed by hand, Frs. Bagnoli and Cavallini are transported to the hospital in Weihui, about 25 kilometers away, where they are finally able to receive treatment for their wounds.

The body of Fr. Mencattini is disinterred, again through the intervention of the Christian official and placed in a wagon. The next day it is transported to Weihui, where his confreres, the faithful, and also many non-Christians gather to wish him a last farewell.

BISHOP ANTONIO BAROSI
(NOVEMBER 23, 1901 – NOVEMBER 19, 1941)

With wide eyes, a small blond altar boy watches the solemn Mass being celebrated by Bishop Geremia Bonomelli. Absorbed in his thoughts, he follows the movements of the great bishop of Cremona, dressed in the vestments reserved for great occasions. Who knows what passes through the mind of that young boy!

Antonio Barosi, born on November 23, 1901 in Solarolo Rainerio, having moved with his family to Cremona in 1912, often serves Mass at the cathedral and always remains fascinated by the priestly ministry.

He does not delay. In 1913 he enters the diocesan seminary, convinced that he will be a priest to serve his own diocese. But after his first year of high school, he hears the talks of Fr. Silvio Pasquali, a missionary in India, and he is drawn by this new figure who appears in his life.

Thus, on September 27, 1919, he decides to continue his priestly preparation in the Seminary for the Foreign Missions in Milan, soon to be followed by his friends Luigi Martinelli and Angelo Corbani, both of whom will become missionaries, the former in Bengal and the latter in India.

Finally, in 1925, he is ordained a priest and on October 5, he receives his mission cross from the Archbishop of Milan, Cardinal Eugenio Tosi. The next day he leaves for China.

Two months and eighteen days of travel, by the most disparate means. Leaving Genoa on a German ship, he arrives in Hong Kong at the end of October, then reaches Shanghai and from there, after four days on the Blue River, he arrives at Hankou. Finally from Hankou, after a day and a half by train and five days in a Chinese wagon, he is in Jingang, the center of his future mission. "Two months and eighteen days of travel! How many villages I have passed through without ever seeing a cross! It's here that I want to give my life for the adventure of God's reign!" These are the first words of young Fr. Antonio upon his arrival in China.

After two months of studying the Chinese language, still disoriented and inexperienced, he is sent to the district of Dengxian, as assistant to Fr. Massa. He is assigned to work with the students of the Catholic school; they will help him to learn Chinese quickly, since by now he can still barely stammer out a sentence or two.

Besides the difficulty of the language and the new environment, he must immediately face the harsh reality of Chinese communism. Indeed, he writes to the seminarians of Cremona in October of 1927:

> Last July the red army entered victoriously into our province of Henan; our vicariate[1] was the first to be invaded, by more than 70 thousand soldiers, without any order or rules. Our churches and houses were all occupied by soldiers, even the house in Dengxian, in which they left just two rooms for us: a month and five days of living with those brigands who did nothing but insult us and kept shouting, "death to the foreigners!"
>
> These soldiers, on the way to Zhumadian, went by train to Kaifeng, the capital of the province, which was besieged and occupied within a few days. The new regime has become famous everywhere. The Catholic Church is forbidden to have schools. In ours, the large rooms which were just completed were closed and requisitioned by the soldiers, who transformed them into barracks. The same is happening in other resi-

---

[1] Apostolic Vicariates are ecclesiastic regions in mission areas, which have not yet been established as dioceses.

dences of the vicariate. Hurray for socialism! Propagandists have been sent from Kaifeng, speaking of the "sun of the future." As soon as they arrived, they began spreading their doctrine, much of which is against us, against our religion, and against the "slaves of foreigners" (the Chinese Christians). Since the new regime has taken over, we cannot go out without hearing insults, curses, and ridicule. Our ministry is greatly hampered, but we are all still at our posts, and we will stay here until they expel us or kill us. I don't deny that there is a lot of suffering. But I also don't deny that the Lord is always here to help and sustain us.

Let's hope that the Lord will grant us a little peace and tranquility in the midst of such confusion, so that we can do a little good — if nothing else, to support the Christians so that they will not have to abandon the faith they have come to.

It's difficult to say when this chaos will end: there are too many arrogant and selfish people. All of them say that they have come to save the homeland, while it is all too clear that they are really out to enrich themselves and win some fame. All of these bosses, however, agree on one point: Get the foreigners out of China.

After a year things seem to return to normal, but in the winter of 1928-29, a great famine strikes Henan:

It hasn't rained for ten months; there was no harvest in the spring nor in the fall. Here in Dengxian, the rooms of the school are now abandoned by the communists, so Fr. Massa and I decided to open them up to the hungry. Considering our resources, we didn't want to accept more than thirty, but once the door is open, how do you close it again? Now we have more than a hundred. Our resources are depleted, and so we have placed the whole situation in the hands of Providence, and with this confidence we keep on working.

Fr. Barosi devotes himself to finding grain and is able to obtain a good quantity from the Catholic farmers. Thus, the 27-year-old Antonio begins to reveal his knack for organization and diplomacy. But it is precisely when diplomacy has no results that Fr. Barosi demonstrates the quality of his faith. On February 9, 1929, a large band of brigands arrives at Dengxian and inflicts cruel torture on the rich of the city, hoping to get large sums of money, all in the view of the fathers, who are threatened with the same treatment if they do not pay in cash. The following morning, with the approach of the regular army, the band seeks refuge in the mountains, taking with them three thousand hostages and the two missionaries, bound and forced to walk in the middle of excited horses. Frs. Massa and Barosi think that it is the end for them. Instead, during the general confusion of the violent battle between the brigands and the regular army, they manage to free themselves from their bonds and hide. After the battle, tired and fearful, they make their way among the dead bodies abandoned on the road and are able to escape. But it seems as if peace never comes for Fr. Barosi.

> After being taken by the bandits, I remained in the district of Dengxian until the beginning of May when I had to return to Kaifeng, to the bishop's residence, because I had contracted smallpox during my last trip to the mission stations. After I got better, I had already prepared my three bags to return to my district when the bishop decided to change my assignment. I didn't want to accept such a delicate office, but in the end, trusting in the Lord, I obeyed. I've now been here for ten months. I need a lot of help from the Lord to carry this heavy cross.

In fact, he is named treasurer of Nanyang, the most important mission of the province. The Christians come to him with their questions, the catechists for books and teaching resources, the fathers for all the needs of their residences, schools, and churches. He must attend to the renters who cultivate the few plots of land owned by the mission, the builders, and craftsmen who work in one station or another. He has to think about the daily bread of the orphans and their education, the sisters who work in the kitchen, the storehouse, assistance to the refugees, the direction of the school for girls. He is also the treasurer of the seminary.

But all of this is not enough: he has to provide food and lodging for passing soldiers and fodder for their animals. To government agents who demand the payment of taxes and absurd customs charges, he must devise a way to pay as little as possible.

He is never overcome. He has no fear even in the face of the immense needs of the people, nor the chronic lack of funds; on the contrary, it seems that the difficulties just inspire him to try the impossible. Fr. Barosi has no sooner assumed his new position in the summer of 1929 than he plans the construction of a new school, in spite of the fact that the mission is facing significant financial problems and renewed persecution toward "all who smell of the Catholic Church." At this very time, which by human standards we would judge to be inopportune, he decides "to open in our main residence of Jingang, the only one not occupied by soldiers, a school which will welcome young people from the different districts who want to study. There was never a second thought, and without considering the difficulties, I devoted myself to starting this much needed school."

The beginnings are modest: small houses built in the Chinese style, recycled furnishings, tables, and wobbly stools. But after a few years, the school reaches a high level of quality, in terms of both the number of students and the education received, so much so that the bishop decides to renovate the entire structure so that it will better respond to new needs.

The Volonteri School (named in honor of the first bishop of Nanyang, Simeone Volonteri) is such a success that the three Catholic universities of Peking, Tianjin and Shanghai agree to accept its graduates without any further entrance examination.

Everything, therefore, seems to be going fine, yet the situation is never easy. On January 18, 1931 Fr. Barosi writes to the seminarians of Cremona:

> For three years we have been living with nervous tension so great that, if not for the special grace of the Lord, we would certainly be worn out completely. Many of our brethren have been captured by brigands and many others have been killed. And unfortunately, the story is not over yet! We live day by day, trusting in the Lord; even here in Jingang we are surrounded by brigands; every night we watch in fear of sudden attacks, not to mention the oppression that the soldiers and the city bosses continually inflict upon us in subtle ways.
>
> I tell you this not so that you might fear the missionary life, but so that you might know the conditions in which we are living and increase your prayers to the Eucharistic heart of Jesus for a little peace and tranquility in this poor country of China. Yet, in spite of all these struggles and trials, the Lord consoles us and blesses our work.

A man of many talents, he must continually take on new responsibilities. He seems tireless and the Pro-Vicar Apostolic[2], Monsignor Pietro Massa, knowing his great abilities, gives him another office:

> Last year the bishop called me in and said to me, "Dear Father, I know that you are already very busy, but I need to ask a big favor of you: take over the position of local vicar[3] in the three western sub-prefectures (an area about half the size of Lombardy [a province of northern Italy the size of West Virginia])." How could I say

---

[2] A Pro-Vicar Apostolic is temporarily in charge of the Apostolic Vicariate while waiting for himself or another to be officially named to the position.

[3] A local vicar is a priest responsible for a part of a diocese or Apostolic Vicariate.

no? In fact, in these days I'm about to go by mule to visit my vicariate. Besides this little job, I'm also in charge of the construction of the cathedral in Nanyang city. As you can imagine, I have to be an engineer, architect, and laborer too. Here you become well versed in all fields. You might think: "How can you keep up with so many things?" You do what you can. Certainly not everything will be done perfectly. Think of what we could do if there were a few more priests! The day begins at 4:00 in the morning and ends at 10:00 at night. And I'm not even mentioning the excursions and trips that have to be done.

It is not only his bishop who asks "favors" of him. In the summer of 1938 the refugees of the villages flooded out by the Yellow River, which has been dammed by the Japanese (or the Chinese?) for strategic reasons, number in the thousands. They ask for food and lodging, health and social assistance. The Japanese advance continues unabated. The wounded are beyond counting, and it is impossible to help everyone; commerce has stopped; prices for basic food staples have gone sky high. The mandarin of the city, overwhelmed by the emergency, requests help from the missionaries, asking them to start a course for nurses, who will be able to help those returning to the front.

Fr. Barosi rises with his usual enthusiasm to the new challenge. He institutes and directs a chapter of the Red Cross and forms a corps of volunteers to carry the wounded and take care of the injured, housing them in the mission residence and nearby fields. It doesn't matter who they are: he tries to help as many as possible.

How many homeless refugees, how many wounded by war or air raids, have found refuge, assistance, and comfort in the Catholic Church! To speak only of our city of Nanyang, in the three dispensaries which we have opened, more than three hundred refugees and wounded are helped every day. During the more than twenty aerial bombings of the city, our first-aid ambulance, staffed by the Canossian Sisters and two or three of the missionaries, is well known for the courage of its workers, who are ready for any sacrifice. All those wounded in the air raids have been taken care of at the expense of the mission.

The bishop's residence at Jingang, a totally Christian town about six kilometers from Nanyang, is a safe refuge for all the important men of the city; even those who hate us, who never lost a chance to hamper our work, now come to ask for help. What a great occasion to make friends: we put our houses at their disposal and everyone is welcome.

The spirit of obedience urges Fr. Barosi to accept still more and greater responsibilities. In 1939, the new bishop Pietro Massa, his first pastor in China, knowing full well that his old assistant in Dengxian has broad shoulders, names him the Pro-Vicar Apostolic. Fr. Antonio begins to substitute for the bishop when he is away, taking care of correspondence with Rome and Milan, handling relations with the authorities, watching over the seminary, the pastoral activities, and the orphanage.

But the situation is becoming more dramatic and grueling: "The terrible trials which are inflicted upon China in these days," he writes, "surpass any previous ones!"

Sometimes I'm tempted to retreat to the quiet of a monastery to think only about the health of my soul… But the apostolate to which we are consecrated and the tasks we have accepted from our Lord immediately call me back to the complete fulfillment of duty, in spite of any difficulty and suffering… I really need your prayers, because in August of last year I was asked by the bishop to take on the delicate position of Pro-Vicar General. I would have just as soon refused, but I had to obey. I feel the weight of the heavy responsibility, especially in these days of such sadness. It's difficult enough to take care of oneself, imagine the task of directing others. Pray for me a lot, so the Lord will provide that which I lack in carrying out my duty for the good of the missionaries and Christians entrusted to my care.

And still it is not enough.

Fr. Barosi is given even more responsibility in a larger field of work. After 45 years of mission, Bishop Giuseppe Tacconi, Apostolic Vicar[4] of eastern Henan, asks the Holy See that the vicariate he founded in 1916 be entrusted to one younger than he. Rome, accepting the request in the spring of 1940, names Fr. Antonio Barosi as apostolic administrator of Kaifeng, capital of Henan and headquarters of the missions, waiting for better times before electing a permanent bishop. Once more, Fr. Antonio obeys.

However, because of difficulties in travel, Bishop Barosi is not able to reach his new area right away. To get to Kaifeng, he must cross the vast bed of the Yellow River and pass through areas which are occupied by the Japanese and those controlled by the Chinese. In fact, this vicariate is divided in two by the river and by the war front. To pass from one part to the other is not only difficult and dangerous, but nearly impossible. Only after two months, due to the efforts of Fr. Vitale, who is well known by the military and civil authorities of both sides, can Barosi begin the journey that will take him to his new destination.

> From Nanyang, my previous vicariate, to Kaifeng, it took twenty days of travel (in peace time it takes only two), using all available means of transportation and facing more than a few dangers, because I had to pass through the Sino-Japanese front. The Lord was with me and I arrived safely.
>
> As soon as I arrived in my new vicariate, I had to go more than 50 kilometers by boat, because after

---

[4] An Apostolic Vicar, normally a bishop, is the person in charge of the mission stations of the vicariate.

breaking through the dikes, the Yellow River had flooded the lowlands in an area 50 kilometers wide and more than 200 kilometers long. Desolation and ruin follow the path of these waters, which flow without any banks through vast areas, submerging fertile fields, destroying villages, hamlets, and cities for hundreds of kilometers, leaving thousands and thousands of poor families in their wake. Many of our most promising Christian communities have been destroyed or dispersed. Eight mission districts are completely or partially under water.

What has really comforted and edified me as I pass through the flooded districts is the spirit of sacrifice of the missionaries entrusted with the care of those territories. In spite of the disaster brought about by the flood, every one of them has remained at his post. With the little money they have been able to receive from benefactors and the International Red Cross, they've truly performed miracles in giving aid amidst such misery. Thus, many people have been saved, who most certainly would have died of exposure and hunger without their help.

His first duty is to visit all the districts under his jurisdiction, to get a complete picture of the Christian communities there, to encourage and console them, and when necessary to reorganize them.

In November of 1941, only the district of Dingcunji remains to be visited. It is located to the south of the city of Luyi, and is almost completely submerged by the waters of the Yellow River which, because of the heavy summer rains, has changed its course and formed a deep, briny lake a few kilometers in area.

The Japanese have pushed forward to Dingcunji three times, but always retreated; the Chinese soldiers have been able to establish complete control of the territory. With good reason, Dingcunji is considered a "no man's land" because in the absence of any central authority, it is continually at the mercy of a wide variety of occupying forces, who rule according to their own will. Since it is a territory bounded by two provinces, when the brigands supported by the communists make raids in the province of Henan, they pass through from their camps in Anhui, and vice versa.

Bishop Barosi fears the hidden dangers of this district, so much so that his visit almost becomes an obsession of dark foreboding. Yet, for the same reasons, he cannot remain safely ensconced in the security of the central house, located in an area controlled by the Japanese, when he knows that his missionaries are exposed to all kinds of threats and dangers.

Thus, on November 10 he leaves by train from Kaifeng, and on November 17, he reaches the Japanese-controlled city of Luyi, where Fr. Zanardi lives. On the morning of November 18, he and Fr. Zanardi leave the city. Before arriving at their destination, they meet up with Fr. Zanella who accompanies them to Dingcunji; they arrive at 4:00 in the afternoon.

The welcome of the people is festive. The presence of the bishop in this moment of crisis provides a great occasion for hope. But joy and happiness always seem destined to last a very short time in China, a country which, at least in these days, seems almost devoid of hope.

FR. MARIO ZANARDI

(OCTOBER 8, 1904 – NOVEMBER 19, 1941)

In Soncino, a village between Cremona and Treviglio, on October 8, 1904, Mario, the second of thirteen children is born to Luigi Zanardi. Perhaps it is from his father, a traveling merchant, that Mario inherits his spirit of initiative and enthusiasm.

Calm, exuberant and expansive at the same time, Mario has a great imagination, so much so that at the parish youth center, he is able to get the other boys interested in music, painting, and mechanics. It is here at the youth center, while taking care of the smaller children, that he begins to develop his spiritual life and priestly vocation. So, at the age of 16, a year after the death of his mother, he decides to enter the diocesan seminary of Cremona.

But little by little the desire to be a missionary begins to grow in him. On February 9, 1925, a Mission Club is officially established at the seminary, with the expressed purpose of instilling missionary awareness in the students. Mario jumps into the activity, and even when he transfers to the P.I.M.E. seminary in Monza after his second year of theology, he never forgets his "roots." He remains so attached to the Mission Club that even from China he would never fail to send letters to its members.

At the P.I.M.E. seminary in Monza, even though he is taken up with his studies, Mario's creativity continues. During his free time, he engages in endless "experiments" with wood and plastic, activities which will be useful to him in the missions, especially in renovating the poor chapels of the Christian communities. He is still enamored by music and the theater as well, so much so that he writes a missionary play, which is performed with great success.

On June 11, 1927 he is ordained a priest. After a few weeks with his family, he leaves for China.

On August 17, on board the steamship *Venezia*, he begins what he calls "my honeymoon," although he is so seasick throughout the entire trip that he cannot even celebrate daily Mass.

The tiring journey lasts three months, during which he has long conversations with the ship's doctor, the Indians confined to fourth class, the baggage handlers, always speaking of the Christian faith. Finally he arrives at Shanghai.

The last stage of the journey, from Hankou to Kaifeng, where he has been assigned, is more exciting. The train has been taken over by communist soldiers and the civilian passengers are forced to ride in the cattle cars, with constant stops along the way. But Fr. Mario consoles himself: "Come what may, this can't be worse than the sea! Besides, what are these discomforts compared to the perilous expeditions of our first missionaries!"

In Kaifeng, his first duty is to learn the language:

> The bishop gave me a book and a teacher. Tomorrow I begin to study! If not for the Lord, I don't believe that I would ever be able to learn Chinese. But with His help and His love, I'm going to learn not only to speak it, but to read it, write it, and even sing it. The Christians here always sing so well!

Only four months later, that which seemed impossible is a reality: he can hear confessions in Chinese and in the Christian communities the faithful marvel that he can speak their language like an old-timer. He knows that he must thank the children for their patience in repeating the pronunciation of simple words to him over and over again.

In 1948, a year after his arrival, the bishop assigns him to the district of Weiche, where everything must be built from scratch. It will require great enthusiasm and good will, and Fr. Mario is just the man for the job.

"Weiche is the place I have been assigned. There really is nothing there, and I need to begin to build from the ground up. But the courage and grace of God are always with me," he writes in June of 1929.

> Oh, the life of a missionary! Those who come must be prepared to suffer and to live a life of exile... In my letters, I describe for you the roses; I don't need to tell you about the thorns, because you can read them between the lines.

Yet, Fr. Mario is not depressed. Weiche is a vast district, with only a very few poor Christians, who are spread out in small, farflung villages, fifteen or twenty kilometers apart, in an area infested with bandits.

> The poetry of the missionary life is nice to see and read about... But I'm also happy to be a missionary in the midst of great difficulties. When my heart is really burdened, I go to church and pour it all out to God. Sometimes He is the only one who understands me... After a while, I can pick up my work and move forward once again.

He prepares catechists, opens schools, starts a health clinic, and according to a fixed schedule, it is he who attends to the sick. "Don't you know? I have become a famous doctor! But those who care for their lives don't place themselves in my care!" In this case, as in others, he demonstrates an exceptional ability in organizing what is most needed to respond to the needs facing the people.

Yet, just when the district is in full swing with activities, he receives the order to transfer to another area. As always, Fr. Mario is ready to obey, but such is not the case among his faithful, who in order to keep him with them, send many requests to the bishop, including a delegation of the most influential and eloquent people of the district. But they do not prevail, and Mario privately prepares for his departure: while another delegation is on the way to Kaifeng, he takes the opportunity to leave. Early in the morning he mounts the motorcycle given to him by the bishop, and heads for Dingcunji, his new assignment. "Others could live there, and I will too!" This was his response when the bishop proposed this district, which no one goes to willingly because it is so far away from the mission, situated on the borders of three provinces and full of bandits. The bishop wants to send him there not only because of his initiative and drive, but also because he is young and a great motorcyclist besides, which can represent safety in that area. Indeed, there would be numerous times when Fr. Zanardi was thankful for the speed of his motorcycle!

On April 30, 1932, for example, while he is instructing the catechists in church, a cry goes up: "Daofei lai (the brigands are coming)!" Aware of the danger, Fr. Mario opens the tabernacle, places the consecrated host in a pyx around his neck, hops on his motorcycle and heads out of the city. The brigands invade the residence, searching for him. They set out to chase him by horse, but luckily he is already long gone.

Many times Fr. Zanardi has to deal with the brigands:

> A large band, which seemed far away, began to approach the town. They are coming, three, five thousand of them. Are they going away, are they coming closer? They're here! From the tower of Dingcunji, you can see a circle of fire; some villages are in flames. Crowds of frantic people scurry to escape. They are at the wall of the city, pounding on the door; when it is finally opened, the streets of the market are teeming with people who are angry and agitated; everyone is looking for family or friends and seeking shelter. Even in the garden, along the surrounding walls, small huts spring up with clay walls and straw roofs.

Fr. Mario becomes a builder to provide shelter to the refugees, and when the storm has passed, all return to their villages to rebuild their huts and start their lives over again.

Fr. Zanardi takes advantage of a calm period to organize a formation course for catechists, visit the villages on motorcycle or bicycle and begin the catechumenate:

In the fall, I began a small catechumenate in the city, but I had a hard time gathering together just a few women. The catechumenate is something new here, and nobody dares to come; a thousand doubts and suspicions keep these poor people away from us at first. There are many obstacle to the Word of God. In my frequent visits to the villages, I see many people, especially the elders, run away as soon as I show up. At first, some people shut their doors and stayed inside, trembling, until I went away. Then after a while, my presence didn't scare them anymore: they were persuaded that the good Lord, whose missionary is a humble servant, is a God of love and goodness... Many hopes are becoming a reality; numerous families are coming to the Christian faith. May the Lord always preserve in them this initial fervor, so needed in this poor land beset by revolutions and brigands.

But even with these good results, trials are never far away, as Fr. Zanardi writes: "In the missions there is suffering, and if not for God's daily sustaining help, no one would be able to live this kind of life." This is the only power he possesses, and it is capable of sustaining him even when he knows that he is placing his life at risk.

Certainly in facing the dangers, he is also helped by his youthful, open character, which could win over even the harshest of the soldiers and bandits.

In the fall of 1936, Fr. Mario is named local vicar of the vast district of Luyi, which includes Dingcunji and some very old Christian communities. He begins to feel very strongly the repercussions of the war, the uncertainty of the situation, the rising prices of commodities, the misery of the people; in the face of this reality, many of the beautiful projects he has in mind are put aside.

The bands of brigands continue to proliferate, spreading ruin and destruction, so much so that Fr. Mario writes to the Mission Club of the Cremona seminary:

You in the peace and serenity of the seminary, we in the midst of dangers and war which sometimes cause us to wish for heaven as a place of sweet rest: we are all united in prayer. We need your love and your prayers for the Lord's mercy and pardon for our many weaknesses... Always follow me with your prayers, especially at this time, since we are in the middle of the horrors of war and bandits.

Indeed, in the spring of 1938, as if the brigands were not enough, the Japanese arrive with their own brand of destruction, violence, and rape. Fr. Zanardi is barely able to get the Chinese sisters and female catechists to a safe place. When the Japanese move on, the brigands return to take over the area, stealing from the poor people what little they have left after being impoverished by the war and the floods of the Yellow River, which reduce the huts of the villages to piles of muck covered with rancid straw.

In an already tragic situation, the following winter brings an immense number of desperate people to the Catholic mission looking for a little food. A bowl of black broth is distributed twice a day, but this depletes the meager resources of Fr. Mario, who desires so much to alleviate, if just a little bit, such suffering.

Fr. Mario, meanwhile, finds himself pushed from one commander to another, until he doesn't know who is in charge anymore. In 1939 he writes: "In three days we have changed masters three times: Chinese, Japanese and brigands, one after another plundering the last supplies of provisions... We live every day completely in the hands of the Lord." This is the power which enables him to continue and even to find reasons for joy.

In the summer of 1939, while the Japanese are occupying the city for the third time, Fr. Mario receives a tandem bicycle, a gift from his friends in Soncino. No gift could have been more appreciated! Now he can finally travel together with the catechist, who is also the altar server, secretary, interpreter, advocate in quarrels between Christians and non-Christians, and, in the absence of Fr. Mario, even a judge.

With the tandem, Fr. Zanardi can take everything he needs for the celebration of the Mass, for catechesis, and evangelization activities: books, devotional objects, pamphlets. The Christian communities can be visited more often and at Christmas time he can more easily get to different communities to celebrate the Mass. He is truly happy!

A tandem bike: a dear gift which reminds him of his faraway homeland, to which he is still very attached. Happy to have been able to put together a rudimentary radio, he can now follow events in Italy, as he gets up at 3:00 a.m. to catch an Italian news program. This is a great sacrifice for him. To wake up again in the morning, he not only has to use two alarm clocks but he also orders one of the domestics to knock on his door.

> Yet, you who live with modern conveniences cannot even imagine what sweet company that radio is to me, as it brings me news of home. Yesterday, I had the good fortune to hear the pope, and I can tell you that it was a great comfort for me to hear his sweet voice in this immense country of China.

Strong, spiritual, happy, but also quite sensitive and affectionate for his family, Fr. Mario maintains strong emotional bonds and is not able to hide his homesickness for very long. On June 3, 1940, he writes to his family:

> Yesterday, my spirit was sad and as gray as the sky. I thought about all of you, of things past and present; of my friends who have died or who have lost their way. I read your long letter, which reminds me of so many things, twenty years distant by now, and with such memories, my eyes filled up with tears. I couldn't keep from crying. I stayed awake until dawn. Then, finally, I was able to sleep.

1940 begins with many problems, unfortunately all too familiar ones. There seems to be no hope. "Send me what you can: the misery is great here; just leaving the house brings tears to your eyes."

In the fall however, there is a great consolation. Bishop Barosi, his fellow citizen and classmate, arrives in Kaifeng. They are finally able to embrace after 15 years! Together, they celebrate the centenary of Blessed Jean Gabriel Perboyre, a French missionary martyred in Henan in 1840.

A year later, when Bishop Barosi decides to visit Dingcunji, Fr. Zanardi accompanies him. On July 18, not having received any alarming news, and even though Fr. Zanardi knows that in this district, considered "no man's land," the Italians are not appreciated, they leave early in the morning on the tandem bike, followed by two domestics on bicycle. Both are aware of the danger, yet Fr. Mario is happy for the chance to see old friends. Along the way they meet Fr. Zanella and all three continue together to Dingcunji; they arrive at 4:00 in the afternoon and find Fr. Lazzaroni waiting for them.

Everything seems peaceful. But the general situation is so tense and confused that no one can ever tell what the next day will bring.

FR. BRUNO ZANELLA

(AUGUST 27, 1909 – NOVEMBER 19, 1941)

Bruno Zanella, born on August 27, 1909 in Piovene di Vicenza, moves with his family to Povegliano di Treviso when he is seven years old. Very soon, however, with his father off to war, the Zanella family is forced to flee during "the Days of Caporetto," when the Austrians defeat the Italian army. Escaping during the night, Bruno, his mother, brothers and sisters, travel through Italy as refugees, until they are finally able to settle in Castelvetrano, in the Province of Trapani.

Once peace is restored, the Zanellas are able to return to Povegliano where they are reunited with their father. He, however, ravaged by the long years of war, dies in March of 1919.

The family is large and needs all the help it can get. As soon as he is finished with elementary school, Bruno becomes an apprentice mechanic. He works until late at night; yet before going to bed he never fails to remind his mother to wake him up in time to serve the Mass before going to work. His missionary vocation is born in work and prayer.

Just at this time, the bishop of Treviso, Andrea Longhin, offers the Institute for Foreign Missions the care of St. Martin parish, in the middle of the city, so that the rectory can become the site of a small seminary. Thus, on October 1, 1923 the missionaries of the Seminary for Foreign Missions open a minor seminary in Treviso, and Bruno Zanella is one of the first students.

Since he is not very accustomed to the use of pen and paper, Bruno does not find it very easy to study. Yet, if he has not been endowed with great academic ability, he makes up for it by force of will and a lot of common sense. These enable him to apply himself to his studies with seriousness and dedication, even though he also suffers from poor health, which often causes him to miss some lessons. Still, he succeeds in completing his seminary studies, not only with good grades, but also having won the sympathy and friendship of his classmates because of his openness and dedication.

In October of 1933, as a student of theology, he moves to Ducenta, to help out in the care of younger seminarians. Two years later, on September 21, 1935, in the Milan Cathedral, he is ordained a priest. The following year, Bruno writes to his family: "I am going to China, the land of my dreams!" He is assigned to Kaifeng, the capital of Henan.

The missionaries will leave from different locations, depending upon their destinations, but a common departure ceremony is held on July 30, 1936 at St. Maria alla Fontana in Milan. Giuseppe Tacconi, bishop of Fr. Bruno's future mission, presides at the liturgy and confers the mission cross. On September 2, Fr. Zanella leaves from Genoa with two companions, heading for China.

An astute observer, he describes in his letters precise details about the places he sees during the journey and his own feelings. At Port Said, Suez, and Aden he is fascinated by the Muslim world; in Bombay, he stands open-mouthed before the "Tower of Silence," where the Parsi expose the bodies of their dead to birds; in Colombo, capital of modern-day Sri Lanka, he is disturbed to see a fanatic who, during a procession in honor of the divinity, throws himself under the wheels of a wagon, killing himself. And then there is a curious, and at the same time embarrassing, episode. In Shanghai, the customs official, worried about drugs entering the country, searches every foreigner, and discovers suspicious envelopes in Fr. Zanella's luggage. He insists on tasting the contents. When he does so, however, he finds that it is simply the powdered laxative which Fr. Bruno must always carry with him.

Finally, the three missionaries reach Kaifeng. Their hearts are filled with joy, and they would like to get to work right away. But, like everyone else, they must first tackle the language. Fr. Bruno spends an entire year at the regional house, studying Chinese. In his first letter to his mother, he writes: "The tones you have to make to pronounce these characters are unimaginable … sometimes the pronunciation is downright incomprehensible!" Still, in this effort too, his strong will sustains him, and at the end of the year he is able to converse relatively well.

In June the Chinese lessons are over and the students are anxious to receive their assignments. Bishop Tacconi calls in Fr. Zanella, and rather than sending him out to a mission district, assigns him to the city.

> The temperature is 100 degrees in the shade; no one dares to go outside in the afternoon. Even the farmers work only in the early morning and in the evening. In the city, all you do is sweat, drink tea, and fan yourself! I always keep my Chinese book at hand (this study is never really finished) and patiently bide my time.

In September Fr. Bruno is informed by the bishop that he will soon go to the mission of Fr. Filippin, as his assistant. But the plan is not carried out. The frequent raids of the brigands in that district worry the bishop, who does not want to expose Fr. Bruno, just 28 years old, to danger.

Seventy kilometers southwest of Kaifeng, the city of Zhongmou is already under the control of the Japanese, and the Chinese pastor of the Christian community there finds himself in a difficult position amidst the dissension between the Chinese and Japanese. Fr. Zanella is sent to help him and to defend him before the Japanese authorities.

After only six months, however, Fr. Bruno is given a new assignment. In the district of Yejigang Fr. Lanzano has been sick for some time, and needs medical attention, so the bishop sends Fr. Zanella there on a temporary basis. Even though he doesn't know how long he will be there, he begins immediately to visit and assist the Christian communities of his new district. In addition, he must go back and forth to the nearby city of Lanfeng to help the resident Chinese priest, who is being bullied by the Japanese. Fr. Bruno is able to develop a good relationship with the invaders. He opens a center for the sick and hungry in his residence, and puts at their disposal everything he possesses. The Japanese admire him so much that they contribute to the assistance of the refugees, sending numerous cases of army rations to them.

October 27, 1940. The missionaries have just finished their retreat and are about to receive their orders from the new superior, Bishop Antonio Barosi. Fr. Bruno is hoping to receive a permanent assignment.

The bishop has in mind for him the farthest and most difficult district, often afflicted by brigands and now flooded by the Yellow River: Dingcunji. Fr. Bruno knows that he is taking on a heavy burden, but he accepts. "I responded with a forced yes," he writes to his mother, almost reproving himself for not having answered the bishop with more enthusiasm.

A grateful Bishop Barosi assigns Fr. Lazzaroni as his co-worker, promises to visit him soon, and assures him that he will find very good Christians there.

On November 6, 1940, after a long and difficult journey, he arrives at his mission. Wasting no time, he begins immediately to make an inspection tour of the different communities, accompanied by his assistant and his predecessor, Fr. Piccinini, who gives him the information he needs about the area.

They return to Dingcunji after 15 days, and Fr. Piccinini leaves for his new post. The two missionaries wait for Bishop Barosi, who is in Luyi for the centenary of the martyrdom of Blessed Perboye, to keep his promise. However, due to an urgent call to Shanghai, he must postpone his visit. So Frs. Zanella and Lazzaroni continue their visits of the Christian communities: by boat in the flooded areas, by bicycle, and on foot.

On January 13, 1941, Fr. Bruno leaves for Kaifeng, having been called by Bishop Barosi, who has just returned from Shanghai. Not yet up to making another long journey (it is 300 kilometers to Dingcunji), the bishop still wants to know how the work is going and to hear first-hand about the missionary life in the "district of the brigands, no man's land." Once again he renews his promise to visit.

Fifteen days later, Fr. Zanella returns to his mission and begins to prepare his people for the sacrament of confirmation, which Bishop Barosi will administer.

Finally it is November. It seems that there are no more obstacles to the arrival of the bishop; but Fr. Bruno, knowing the difficulties of the journey, hastens toward Luyi to meet him. On November 18, as he approaches the city, he finds the bishop and Fr. Zanardi already on their way, so he goes with them back to Dingcunji, where Fr. Lazzaroni is waiting.

Finally, the bishop is about to arrive.

FR. GEROLAMO LAZZARONI

(SEPTEMBER 27, 1914 – NOVEMBER 19, 1941)

Colere: a tiny village in the province of Bergamo, located in the enchanting Valley of Scalve, on the north slope of the Presolana Mountains.

It is early 1900. The families of this area, in order to survive, cultivate some vegetable gardens, grow a little hay, and rent one or two cows in the wintertime so that they can be sure of a little milk in the long, cold season. Often, however, it is not enough, and the head of the family must go elsewhere in search of work.

Such is the life of the Lazzaroni family. Gerolamo, from an early age, helps to collect the potatoes, cut and bale the hay, and herd the sheep to pasture. With his three older brothers, he has to help his mother keep the family going, because his father leaves for long periods of time to find work as a miner in Australia.

Thus, when Gerolamo confides to his mother his desire to enter the seminary, it is inevitable that the response will be a terse no. Really, it would be unthinkable; just the cost of his travel to the city of Bergamo is more than the family budget can handle. It's best if he simply puts this dream aside. There is no way the poor Lazzaroni family can pay for his room and board nor the required uniform (accustomed as he was to wearing patched pants and sandals). His mother hopes that this is just a passing phase.

But in 1927, after the return of his father for good, Gerolamo (now 13 years old) brings up the topic again. The presence of his father assures some stability for the family, and the savings brought from Australia can provide a significant, if limited, respite from financial worries. Thus, in November of 1927, with a third-grade education and a little bit of Latin picked up from his pastor, Gerolamo leaves Colere for the diocesan seminary of Bergamo.

Used to long walks in the mountains, always out in the fresh air, at first he finds seminary life difficult. Those long hours sitting at his desk and listening to things which are incomprehensible to him sometimes seem like a prison sentence. He can't sing to the squirrels as he used to do while collecting wood with his brothers. He has to stay closed up in a classroom, while the sky is blue and he feels like running outside, with the breeze flowing through his hair, climbing mountains, scrambling to the top of Presolana.

With all the difficulties of studies and community life, he feels like giving up and going home. But his vocation cannot be burst like a soap bubble; he trusts in the Lord and often remembers the words of his pastor: "Nothing good can be accomplished in life without effort and sacrifice." With his head in his hands, then, he returns to his books, sure that even now he is already in God's service.

Eventually, the environment and people, so different from his own culture, begin to become familiar. He is assigned to lead treks through the mountains, to organize soccer games, and to fill the evenings with activities designed to overcome homesickness. Lively and humorous, he invigorates the seminary with his wit. He also progresses in his studies, so much so that when classmates do not understand some topic, they come to him for an explanation.

In the meantime, during his high-school years, his desire to be a missionary grows, and in 1935 he transfers to the P.I.M.E. seminary in Genoa, and then on to Milan. A few months before his priestly ordination in 1938, both of his parents die within a short time of each other. It is a heavy blow for him, since he is so attached to his family, but even in this difficult situation, he trusts completely in the Lord. To those who offer condolences, he replies: "The Lord has already granted them their reward for the sacrifice of offering their son to Him for the missions."

Ordained on September 24, 1938 in the Milan Cathedral, he celebrates his first Mass in Colere. At sunset, his friends give him a great surprise. In the valley, lights begin to flicker and soon take the shape of an enormous chalice and host.

At the age of 24, he is informed of his destination: together with his classmate Valentino Corti he is assigned to the mission of Hanzhong in the Chinese province of Shaanxi, the most distant of the missions of P.I.M.E. And so, on August 16, 1939, he leaves Genoa for a destination that he will never reach because of the Sino-Japanese war.

After disembarking at Shanghai, he reaches Kaifeng and stays there with the other new missionaries for a year of language study. His joviality and love for jokes do not diminish a bit: "My professor is a good Catholic. Too bad he can only speak Chinese! To help us understand his baffling sayings, he moves right and left, he sits on the ground or climbs up on a chair, he acts blind, he jumps and dances; it's all quite entertaining." To break the monotony of studies, the fathers sometimes make little trips outside of the city, visiting one Christian community or another. The elusive language remains a torture for Fr. Gerolamo, even though he is beginning to enjoy its beauty. When he listens to a Chinese telling a story, he pays more attention to the way of speaking than to the content, marvelling at the ease with which every detail and shade of meaning is expressed. Soon he will try to preach, and will then be a "true" missionary. This is his great desire, as he expresses in a letter to his sister:

> Pray that I learn this language as well as possible so that I can do much good here, where the Lord wants me to be. Every day I become more aware of how unprepared I am for the mission entrusted to me by the Lord. It is not beautiful homilies that convert souls, but rather all the daily sacrifices that Providence places before us.

In June of 1940 the year of language study is over, and all the missionaries leave the regional house for their respective missions. But Frs. Lazzaroni and Valentino Corti, assigned to the vicariate of Hanzhong (Shaanxi), cannot leave. The long trip is dangerous even under normal conditions; now, because of the Sino-Japanese war, it is practically impossible. Fr. Gerolamo must wait. But he feels like a fish out of water.

I am well here, and far away from any danger, but I am not at my post. I want so much to set out for my mission, far away and isolated, toward the border of Tibet, where you can find the true and authentic China of Confucius... I continue to hope that a way is opened to Hanzhong. Ah, if only I could go by bicycle!

The enthusiasm of youth is not diminished by the prospects of the risks to be faced, so much so that if it were up to him, he would leave for his mission by any means of transportation.

Unfortunately, though, he is not able to do so, and while waiting for better times, he stays in Kaifeng. Finally, he is assigned to the mission of Dingcunji, of which Fr. Bruno Zanello has just been named pastor. The two of them leave the city together.

After going a short way by train, no one knows how the journey can continue. There are no roads anymore, only flooded areas crossed by raft to avoid the slimy, muddy ground. Having conquered the 300 kilometers to Dingcunji, Fr. Gerolamo writes: "I traveled by train, by bicycle, on foot, by boat, and by ox cart. But I have finally arrived where the Lord wants me to be!"

Fr. Edoardo Piccinini, the former pastor of the district, now assigned to Taikang, is there to meet them and to give his successors all the necessary information about the area. Thus, just two days after arriving, the three missionaries are on the road again, to visit the different Christian communities. Even though he is in the midst of much desolation because of the flooding, the brigands, and the war, Fr. Gerolamo is happy to be living the dream held so dear during his years of study and prayer.

Back in Dingcunji, Fr. Lazzaroni is given the job of teaching catechism to the children every day, during the last hour of school.

Gerolamo likes the Chinese children. It hasn't been that long since his own childhood, and he understands very well what it is like to be without adequate shoes in the winter, or to walk in a rainstorm without an umbrella, or to be unable to replace a notebook which is filled up. He loves these children, understands them, and is ready to give his life for them.

He writes on January 2, 1941:

> I spent Christmas here at Dingcunji, while Fr. Bruno was about 30 kilometers away. More than 200 Christians came for the celebration, and all of them wanted the sacrament of confession; then they participated in midnight Mass... I was dead tired when I walked out of the church at noon, and there were even more people waiting. All of them stopped by the mission house to give their Christmas greetings and to bring me a gift: a bag of sweets, a chicken, a dozen eggs, a homemade cake ... and to think that they have barely enough to keep from starving! Certainly if I did not accept, they would be offended. I redistributed everything to the children... So, in general, I'm doing well here. I miss news of the Western world, but the next time I go to Kaifeng (300 kilometers away), I will bring my radio, and then things will be even better!

He is content with little and still knows how to be humorous. In a letter to his brother-in-law he writes: "My beard is not growing very well, because I don't have anyone to pull on it. Occasionally I try to pull on my pastor's beard, but he is too good to respond in kind." And he adds: "I know that you are a good bricklayer, but did you know that I am a good road builder? If you want to go to Heaven, you have to build the road yourself."

This has more than symbolic meaning for him; he really does have to repair the roads on many occasions. He writes in March of 1941: "Last week I redid part of the road which I had just repaired five months ago, when I got here. Then it was nothing more than an extension of the Yellow River; now it is passable for a few kilometers, but the rest cannot be fixed."

Meanwhile, the suffering increases. "I am very happy with my Christians, and I feel so sorry for their misery," he writes in the same letter.

In autumn, they planted some corn. But now in the spring, with the melting snow, the river has overflowed causing immense damage. Except for some rare exceptions, they live in miserable, dark, smoky hovels, open to the four winds, which blow strongly on some nights. Food is scarce and miserable. Now that the Japanese have taken away the rice, there is not even that. The poorest in Europe are richer than these Chinese.

He suffers with the people and for the people. "This is a real no-man's-land. As if all the rest weren't enough, there are the Japanese troops, the Chinese soldiers, and the brigands dressed in camouflage. All of them do nothing but harass the people."

The camouflaged brigands — these are the real rulers of the territory. They make themselves at home, and no one tries to get rid of them. It is easier to ignore the problem and to pretend that it doesn't exist. The district of Dingcunji is on the border of three provinces, each of which passes the responsibility to the other, claiming that the area is not under its authority. Thus, it is here that all the outlaws congregate: deserters, mercenaries, common criminals, all gathered in unruly, undisciplined groups, pushed toward violence by hunger and unrest. In a word, they are men to fear. Still, despite this situation of extreme insecurity, the missionaries remain and travel here and there amidst the danger, in solidarity with their people.

Fr. Gerolamo is not afraid of the difficulty, the struggles, and the dangerous trips: he is strong, courageous, and not the type of person to suffer oppression passively. Yet even the strongest must sometimes give in to the events surrounding them and to the prudence of "weakness."

On November 18, Fr. Lazzaroni is alone at Dingcunjji. Fr. Zanella has gone to meet the bishop. In the little community, everything is prepared. A rainbow at the entrance of the village is a sign of hope.

MARTYRDOM AT DINGCUNJI
(NOVEMBER 19, 1941)

It is November 19, 1941, an autumn Sunday afternoon. The first winds out of the north chill the air. But in Dingcunji there is an air of festivity, in spite of the gray skies. Bishop Barosi is here for a pastoral visit. Every Christian has done as much as possible so that the village, notwithstanding the difficult times, appears worthy of this solemn occasion. This is the first time that a bishop has ever visited this community in person.

The pastor, Fr. Zanella, has insisted that the bishop come to confer the sacrament of Confirmation. The Confirmation candidates of other nearby villages also gather in Dingcunji, staying with friends or relatives, and by Saturday there is a lot of commotion as people arrive and try to get settled. Those too far away, and those who would have had to travel through areas flooded by the Yellow River, will be visited on Sunday afternoon by the bishop, accompanied by Frs. Zanella, Lazzaroni, and Zanardi.

Once the confirmation liturgy is completed in the morning, the bishop spends some time with the catechists, the confirmands, and their relatives. Then everyone goes to lunch. At 1:00 an official with ten soldiers enters the residence of the missionaries. After putting out the Chinese Christians, he closes the door and sets a troop of well armed soldiers to guard it. A kind of curfew is imposed upon the whole village of Dingcunji.

Fr. Pollio (who would become the bishop of Kaifeng in 1947) describes what happens in the first pages of his diary, then sends a more detailed account to the superior general of P.I.M.E., Bishop

Mario Balconi. From this account we know the particulars of the homicides.

The official and the soldiers, as soon as they enter the house, ask for Fr. Zanella, who comes forward immediately. The soldiers take him to a room in front, where the fathers had barely finished lunch, on the pretext of asking him some questions. Almost simultaneously, they ask for Fr. Lazzaroni, who is led to the sacristy, told not to move, and is left with guards at the door. The official and the soldiers go directly to the room where the bishop is chatting with the other missionary. Bishop Barosi has an identification card issued by the Japanese, a pass which enables him to move about in the areas controlled by Japanese forces. This is the excuse the soldiers use to accuse all four missionaries of being "spies of the enemy and agents of capitalism." The bishop tries kind words with the official, but at his signal, the soldiers bind Bishop Barosi and Fr. Zanardi hand and foot. Fr. Zanardi begins to shout. Immediately they are dragged to the church and thrown to the ground, their mouths and ears stuffed with paper.

At this point the soldiers bind the eyes of one of Bishop Barosi's domestics, Han, who has come with the fathers from Kaifeng, so that he could not testify to what would happen next. The cook, however, is in a position to know the details. He is in the kitchen, hiding in fear in a corner, covered with straw and firewood. From here, he witnesses the martyrdom of Fr. Zanella. The soldiers bring Fr. Bruno outside the room, and pour boiling water and oil into his mouth from large containers. Between life and death, the father cries out often in a language the servant doesn't understand, and other times insists that they have no weapons or money. With a loud howl he implores the help of Bishop Barosi and Fr. Zanardi, but receives no response. Finally the soldiers, after making him drink the boiling water and oil many times, leave his body, unconscious or dead, in the small courtyard. No one can say whether Fr. Zanella dies in that courtyard, or at the bottom of the well into which he would later be thrown. The cook, meanwhile, sees that the soldiers are forcing the bishop and Fr. Mario toward the other courtyard.

After looting the house of any precious or useful items, the soldiers leave Dingcunji around 5:00 PM. They disappear into the darkness on boats, while freezing rain begins to fall in the quiet of the evening. Only at this point do the Christians approach the residence. They force open the door and find Han tied up in the entranceway. They free him and begin to search for the fathers. They call out, but receive no response. There is no trace of blood nor of bodies in the ransacked house. As yet, they do not suspect what has happened, especially since they had not heard any gun fire. Against all hope, they think that the missionaries have been taken hostage. They continue to call out, to search every corner, but find nothing. Finally, someone notices that the wall around the well is crumbled and bricks are completely obstructing its mouth (this would not be a difficult task, since Chinese wells are very narrow). They look on silently; no one dares to reveal the suspicions of their hearts: there must be something under those bricks. They begin clearing them away and the bodies of the victims appear. With long bamboo poles and a hook, they try to bring the bodies up. The first is Fr. Zanella, then Fr. Zanardi, and then Bishop Barosi. It is already late and they have not yet been able to find the body of Fr. Lazzaroni. They work fruitlessly for some more hours, and then give up for the night. At the first light of dawn, they are finally able to recover the body of Fr. Lazzaroni, who almost certainly was thrown into the well alive.

Fr. Gerolamo Lazzaroni was 27 years old, and only two years in the mission; Fr. Bruno Zanella was 32, in the mission for five years; Fr. Mario Zanardi had just turned 37 and had been in the mission for 14 years; Bishop Antonio Barosi was 40 years old, of which 16 were spent in China.

FR. CARLO OSNAGHI

(OCTOBER 26, 1899 – FEBRUARY 2, 1942)

The sun has long since set on this faraway prairie of Yejigang. It's very cold on the night of February 1, 1942, with drizzling rain driven by a strong north wind. Fr. Carlo Osnaghi stirs restlessly on his cot.

He has suffered insomnia since his youth, and even in the mission he has spent many a sleepless night. The nighttime hours are long, but also very "fruitful," especially for one who slips easily into memories. Fr. Carlo remembers the nights spent bent over tattered notebooks, correcting Latin translations and math problems. That was in 1924 when, as soon as he arrived in Kaifeng, the bishop assigned him to teach in the seminary. He had never imagined, during his own years of formation, that his missionary life would consist of spending time with Cicero and the Pythagorean theorem.

Now, however, he has something different to keep him awake. Indeed, it is not a night spent in study nor the preparation of classes, and his worry has nothing to do with the undisciplined students who laugh irreverently when he, the professor, mangles a monosyllabic Chinese word, changing its meaning completely.

No, it is the voices coming from the other corner of the hut that give him no peace. Loud and angry voices, fortified by who knows how many glasses of rice wine, voices suggesting greater violence to come. They curse him, the bishop, and all the priests who have so little consideration for his life that they will not pay the ransom demand. He tries not to think about it. He nudges the Chinese catechist, his unlucky companion, who continually stares at him with wide eyes. He can't sleep either. He knows very well that at any moment their captors could decide their fate. Only Huang San, the 12-year-old boy lying nearby, seems blessed with sleep. Why should he worry? Surely he knows that his father, the eminent mandarin of the area, will do something to come and save him or will pay the last cent required for his release. Fr. Carlo, on the other hand, knows that it is much different for him. He is sure that his superiors are doing everything they can to free him from this prison and that negotiations have gone on for several days; but he is just as sure that there is no way his confreres can come up with the 500,000 dollars required to pay for his release.

The anxiety grows and grows. Once again he turns to look at his catechist. He is filled with admiration for this simple and courageous Christian who insisted on following and staying with him, even when he was given the chance to leave freely.

The brigands holding them hostage begin to argue. Fr. Carlo hears his name among the shouts.

His nervousness increases. He looks through the pockets of his pajamas, the same ones he was wearing when he was taken away in the middle of the night. He finds his rosary and anxiously begins to pray the Hail Mary. His tired eyes look out into emptiness.

Even though he has been held captive for twenty days, he still cannot believe that this is happening to him. In his mind, he still hears those insistent knocks on the door of his mission house in Yejigang.

It was the night of January 12 when, jumping out of bed, he rushed to the door to see who was in such urgent need. For a moment he thought that it had to do with a request for last rites. But as soon as he found his glasses and his sight became accustomed to the dark of the night, he knew that this wasn't the case. A large group of armed men immediately grabbed him and tied him up.

Then they were in the house, tearing it apart. They turned the church upside down as well, stealing anything they could. Then the missionary, the catechist and the young boy were brought to a hut in an open field on the northeast border of Henan, so that at the slightest hint of danger the band would be able to escape easily into another province.

Fr. Carlo, still dazed and unbelieving, let himself be dragged away without any resistance.

Often during his eighteen years in China he had thought about, and even desired, a violent death like that of Jesus, for the sake of the Gospel. And this thought amazed him, not so much because it was out of place, but because it was so out of character with his general timidity. How could he, who was "afraid of his own shadow," find the courage necessary for martyrdom? But with the passage of time, he learned to live with these feelings and to allow his hidden determination to emerge. He knew well that he was no hero, and in fact heroism never seemed important to him. It was enough for him to be a good missionary, and that's all. And so he discovered the silent martyrdom which daily accompanies that acceptance of one's own fragility.

Meanwhile the rosary flows quickly through his fingers. He has always had a great fear of the brigands. His bishop knew this, and in 1926, after only a few months in the district of Yuanzhai, which was teeming with armed bands, he called Fr. Osnaghi back to Kaifeng and appointed him as assistant pastor at the Cathedral and chaplain of the orphanage.

But this time there is no "emergency exit." He cannot think about what might have been, but must face the reality before him. And the brigands engaged in heated debate are that reality now. He is in their hands. His thoughts go to his confreres who have just been killed in Dingcunji.

A shiver runs through his body. He thinks back upon those tragic events, how the news reached Kaifeng at the beginning of the year that his four confreres had been murdered. He had known Fr. Zanella especially well, because he had worked in Yeijigang; in fact, in 1937, he was the one Fr. Osnaghi was sent to replace.

What a shock to hear that story! Fr. Carlo could not help but reveal his feelings to his mother, to whom he was quite attached:

> We are all at a loss. It almost seems like a dream. Let us
> pray that the blood of these victims will be the last.
> From heaven may they look down upon all of us who
> remain in this troubled land, so full of thorns, and pro-

tect us. But if it must be, may they give us the strength
to die as generously as they did.

His mother — while he continues to pray, her image becomes
more and more clear to him. He has written to her often, confiding in
her every joy, difficulty, and worry. In 1930, after various experiences
in Kaifeng, he was sent to Fengjiao, the center of three ancient Christian villages, not far from the city of Luyi. With his mother he rejoiced
about his Christian communities and spoke to her about his pastoral
work. He shared his dreams with her. He liked it there a lot and could
have stayed there forever. Instead, in November of 1937, he was transferred to the district of Yejigang, once a flourishing market, when the
Yellow River flowed near. It had been aptly called "Pheasant Hill," even
though now not a single pheasant was to be found, only poverty and
squalor, caused by the river's change of course.

These were difficult times for Fr. Carlo. His memory goes to the
numerous villages in the different communities, the long trips he had
to made on foot, since his bad eyesight would not allow him to go by
bicycle, to the nights spent in seedy inns or among the poor Christians.
And then, upon his return to the mission house, there was always some
surprise, like the time he found it completely looted by thieves.

But these physical problems were not the only ones.

Because of the intensification of the Sino-Japanese war in 1937,
Fr. Carlo was increasingly seen as a dangerous enemy, just for the fact
that he was a foreigner. Any kind of hospitality began to disappear, to
be replaced by suspicion and fear on the part of anyone he met. Yet, he
never stopped loving these people: "Poor, unhappy China! How much
we, your latest apostles, love you; we're ready to undergo anything to
save you from the abyss. And if God desires victims of expiation, here
we are!"

His mind returns to that period of time when he found it difficult
to see and feel the presence of God, as he confided to his mother: "To
make matters worse, sometimes God seems to be hidden, and I come
into His presence like a piece of wood, without any fervor at all. This is
to suffer a slow martyrdom of the soul. But I accept any trial, if only I

might have the grace to truly love God."

While the strong wind continues to blow through the walls of the hut, his prayers become more subdued. No voices are heard now. Maybe everyone is asleep. Even the catechist is drowsy. The first light of dawn slowly advances through the whirlwind of fine sand whipped up by the wind along the Yellow River.

It is February 2, 1942. The brigands have made their decision. It is useless to wait any longer. Suddenly, Father sees the door burst wide open. "Get up, now! Hurry! Today you will be set free!" He doesn't know whether to believe his ears. The other two hostages, filled with hope, have already scrambled to their feet. The three prisoners are led out into the open and begin walking, escorted by their kidnappers. Fr. Osnaghi feels light, as if a great weight has been lifted off of him. Soon he will be free again. But not very far from the hut, they stop in front of a large freshly dug pit, two meters deep.

> At a signal from the chief of the brigands, they suddenly tied the hands and feet of the three prisoners; the young Huang began to shout and cry. Meanwhile, with a fierce kick they sent Fr. Osnaghi rolling into the pit; with a second kick they rolled in the cook (the catechist, according to other sources), who fell on top of Fr. Osnaghi, and they immediately began to cover the pit with earth. Huang San has repeatedly affirmed that Fr. Osnaghi, finding himself tied up at the front of the pit and seeing no means of escape, let forth with a loud wail, in which he shouted some foreign words and some words in Chinese, calling his mother. And while the brigands were burying the hostages, while the earth was piling up upon their bodies, Fr. Osnaghi and the catechist continued to cry out, until little by little, their cries ceased. *(From the diary of Fr. G. Pollio)*

Huang, the son of the mandarin, is released.

HONG KONG:

THE DIFFICULT STEPS
OF A LITTLE GIANT

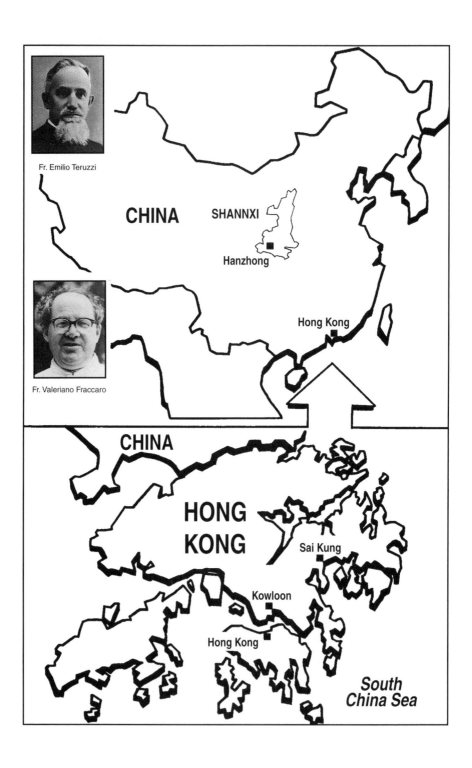

Fr. Emilio Teruzzi

CHINA

SHANNXI

Hanzhong

Fr. Valeriano Fraccaro

Hong Kong

CHINA

HONG KONG

Sai Kung

Kowloon

Hong Kong

South China Sea

INTRODUCTION

By Fr. Giancarlo Politi, PIME

ON JUNE 30, 1997, HONG KONG WAS ONCE AGAIN INCORPORATED into China proper. Since 1841 it had been a small British colony located on the southwest coast of China. It is comprised of the originally ceded island of Hong Kong; the small Kowloon peninsula which, together with Stonecutter's Island, was added to the treaty in 1860; and a larger area of the mainland, called New Territories, leased for 99 years, beginning in 1898. The territory had changed radically over the last 150 years. The arid, rocky, inhospitable inlet had been transformed into one of the most modern, dynamic and economically vibrant cities of the world.

The Catholic church has shared in the evolution of the city. Initially nothing more than a military chaplaincy for the Irish soldiers of the British army, it has slowly transformed into the present dynamic diocese[1]. In the meantime, however, following the events of 1949, the church lost much of its territory within the borders of the People's Republic.

Those events of 1949, culminating in the proclamation of the New China, were most significant in the development of Hong Kong. The installation of a new government in Beijing, and especially the

---

[1] Even before the conclusion of the so called "unequal treaty" whereby China ceded Hong Kong to Great Britain, there were soldiers stationed on the island, among which were many Irish Catholics. Initially, their spiritual assistance was handled by priests from the nearby island of Macao; then the mission of Hong Kong was established on April 22, 1891, with missionaries living in the new colony itself.

standoff with the nationalists, sparked a massive influx of refugees into the small colony. This phenomenon would be repeated in 1960, caused by the devastation of the infamous "great leap forward," during which 43 million people were killed.

This influx of refugees caused years of crises, aggravating the already difficult economic situation brought about by the war and the recently concluded Japanese occupation. The policy followed by the local authorities, however, determined the future of the territory to a great extent. The government on the one hand shrewdly maintained an openness to welcome all of those who were pressing against its borders, and on the other hand asked the help and support of non-governmental agencies operating in the territory in confronting the emergency. Among these, the Catholic church, which offered its full cooperation and the service of its qualified members, grew in recognition and esteem before the entire population. Additionally, the majority of the refugees brought with them a history of professional training and serious work habits. All of these factors brought about, in the course of a few years, the complete transformation of the colony into a first class business environment. Hong Kong was thus preparing to take on a strategic role in international politics and economy, offering itself as a mediator between China and the rest of the world. This would determine the fate of the territory during the entire decade of the eighties.

This difficult process, which made Hong Kong the standard of capitalism on the threshold of the largest "proletarian state" in the world, did not leave the population unaffected. Indeed, it is an "open secret" that the communist party, officially banned from the public life of Hong Kong, has always been active there. Its real power was seen in the public strikes organized to coincide with the great ideological campaigns (viz., the cultural revolution of 1966-67) launched by the communist regime beyond its own borders. Beijing, however, had its own reasons for not allowing the local branches of the CCP (Chinese Communist Party) to disturb the public life of Hong Kong beyond certain limits. After all, Hong Kong was, and still is, pouring vast amounts of currency into the exhausted coffers of the bankrupt communist government. It was important, however, to keep the colonial authorities and the people fully aware that their well-being depended solely upon the good will of Beijing, and no one else. To this end, they made shrewd use of local organized crime groups who, in exchange for protection against outside intervention, were expected to render certain services when requested. Public order in Hong Kong, even today, cannot be maintained without the active collaboration of communist Chinese authorities. Moreover, the 1993 declaration released by the Chinese security ministry maintains that organized crime groups will still have a role after 1997, "if they prove themselves to be patriotic."

But to understand fully the events which are described in the following pages, it is necessary to go back in time once more. In the 1940s the north coast of the colony — the districts of Haifeng and Lufeng — was beset with intense political conflicts. In this area, there had already sprung up the first "soviets," the forerunners of that sociopolitical organization which would eventually extend throughout all of China. Their rise had not occurred without violence, and they had put the legitimately constituted authority to flight. The Catholic diocese of Hong Kong had a few foreign missionaries and Chinese priests in these districts. They were much respected by the people for their well organized and effective charitable activities, which provided an alternative to the type of social advances proposed by the soviets.

In those years, communications between Haifeng and Hong Kong passed across the waters of the vast district of Cairn, then not easily accessible by land (from Kowloon). We find Fr. Emilio Teruzzi working here and, during the years of the cultural revolution, Fr. Valeriano Fraccaro as well.

FR. EMILIO TERUZZI

(AUGUST 17, 1887 – NOVEMBER 26, 1942)

Even though the gray skies do not look promising, at least it has stopped raining. For some time now, not a day has gone by without a sudden downpour of rain. In such a situation, it is difficult, if not impossible, to cross the muddy paths which lead to the farflung villages spread out along the rocky coast of Cairn, in the New Territories.

Fr. Emilio, lost in thought while seated on a rocky buttress overlooking the sea, allows himself to be carried by a long wave of sadness. It has been a long time since any boat has come by. Cairn, an ancient market on the seashore, seems deserted. The boats bringing shoppers from nearby villages have suspended their service. There is an air of terror.

It is November 16, 1942. Not yet a year has passed since the December 1, 1941 invasion of Hong Kong by the Japanese army, which quickly defeated the defenders and began occupation. There has been no peace ever since. If misery, famine, and abuses are commonplace in the city, it is even more disastrous and chaotic on the continent. The majority of the occupied regions do not, in fact, allow the Japanese complete control, and many areas frequently return to the hands of the Chinese. Guerrillas, brigands, and communists, all spouting patriotism, take advantage of the confusion to make raids. Every day there are killings, disorder, vendettas, entire villages destroyed.

Fr. Teruzzi, who has just returned to his old mission, is bewildered. He had been pressing the bishop to allow him to return among the Chinese of Cairn, and he is still at a loss to explain whether his insistence was based upon courage or ignorance. Certainly, he felt a duty to return.

He had been in Hong Kong for some time to help Bishop Valtorta in pastoral and charitable activities, but Fr. Emilio was constantly concerned about the two Chinese priests left behind in his parish. For months he had no news, until he learned in the beginning of September that they, together with eight other persons, had been captured and killed by communist guerrillas. At first, he was filled with tremendous anger, a deep sense of resentment and powerlessness, then the strong desire to return and replace them, to continue their work. Who better than he, who knew the place and its dangers, would be able to help those poor, destitute people, left completely to themselves?

The bishop remained undecided for some time, but finally had to give in. His hard words still echo in Fr. Emilio's mind: "But don't go crazy. Remember that you are only there to study the situation. I have no intention of leaving you in Cairn. I recommend, I command, that you be careful not to expose yourself to the danger of capture."

"I'll see what I can do," he remembers as his diplomatic reply, aware of the heightened risks he was about to face. But now, he cannot, in the name of prudence, avoid visiting the villages. They are a part of his life now. He knows each family by name, their joys, their problems. So many, who are now adults, he watched being born. At the same time, they have learned to know him, to accept and respect him. He begins to smile.

With extreme precision, even though many years have passed, the memories of the struggles and fears of those first years in the mission come back to him. Everything was a great unknown; everything caused stress: the language, the culture, the people, even the very landscape. He wrote to a friend in Italy in November of 1914:

> I am in charge of the district, and I sail in a sea of difficulties. I don't know the language, since the dialect generally spoken here is different from the one I studied. I didn't have enough time with my predecessor to receive all the necessary information about the religious, moral, and financial issues of the district. And these are what cause problems for me.

My Christians, miners or fishermen, go almost all day on a little piece of fish and some vegetables. It is not the sheep who sustain the shepherd; he must provide everything for himself and even for them. The district which has been entrusted to my poor care consists of the part of the colony called "New Territories," which is larger than our beloved Brianza. The landscape is splendid, interspersed as it is between the mountains and the sea. But to enjoy the beautiful views you need to endure tiring climbs, and the sea can get quite churned up; so you can imagine what life is like here.

I ask you to say a Hail Mary for me to the Queen of Heaven and the Star of the Sea that if I have to end up as food for the fish, she will grant me the grace to be well prepared for it.

Looking at a map of my district or viewing the area from the top of some mountain and knowing that so many villages are already caught in the shadow of death, my heart is stricken, my feet are anxious, my hands are itching. I want to run and throw myself in among these people, but I must say with the prophet, "I am too young; I don't know how to speak."

All of the Christians of my district are located on a kind of peninsula. There are quite a few of them, since this is the oldest mission. I have 15 chapels to care for, but most of them are falling down and in need of repair. The waters [financial resources] are very, very low; almost completely dried up. These blessed white ants are not content with eating the houses and chapels; they also have to eat the shoes and wallet of the poor missionary.

Then there are the schools, another great drain on the financial waters. I would like for all the children to learn at least their prayers and catechism, but school is not mandatory here. And if we begin to insist more strongly, they respond, "Father, give me the money and my child will study." Here, that's the fastest way to make even the missionary shut up.

Now he wonders once again, where he ever found the courage, not only to persevere in the face of so many moments of discouragement and disillusionment, but also to defend his Chinese people against injustice and abuse. More than once he has felt lost. Like the time when he went forward with plans to build a school on a hill that had been illegally claimed by an influential figure of the area, who stirred up the entire village against him. If not for the intervention of the British police (whom the Chinese feared more than spirits), they certainly would have resolved the issue by tearing him to pieces. One other time, he showed himself unafraid of approaching a band of brigands to secure the release of a hostage. Now he laughs to think about, but he put on such a good act of self-assurance that the ringleader was won over, and the two ended up becoming friends!

Fr. Emilio knows how to make himself accepted, and this is the talent which has helped him in thousands of situations. When he went back to Italy for the twenty-fifth anniversary of his ordination in 1937, his superiors asked him to remain there and serve in the seminary. Thus, his short vacation turned into a two-year stint; and even though his longing for China was great and reentering the world of Italian youth, difficult, once he applied himself to the task, he became not only a rector for the seminarians but also their confidant and friend.

But he knows how to get what he wants as well. That is how, for example, he managed to get back to Hong Kong. He is, however, not a rebel at heart, and for this reason, even though he desperately wanted to go immediately back to his mission in Cairn, he waited for the authorization of the bishop, and accepted in the meantime a series of appointments in the diocesan offices. In fact, he began many activities with Catholic Action in the city and formed new Boy Scout troops, even going along to their summer and winter camps despite his fifty plus years. He also became the diocesan archivist. Actually, he was not new to this type of work; years before he had managed to use his "free time" to organize the files of the mission, which contained precious documents regarding all the missions of China since 1841. He even wrote "A Brief History of the Apostolic Vicariate of Hong Kong."

"But this time I could not insist," Fr. Emilio says to himself as he watches a ray of sun fighting its way through the clouds.

Certainly, his legs are not as agile as they used to be; yet, as long as the mud allows, he will once again walk these well remembered paths. He doesn't fear the guerrillas. The week before, he ran into a small group. "They stopped me and asked a few questions. Realizing that I had neither fangs nor claws, they let me go in peace. We parted like good friends, thank God." He has just written to Bishop Valtorta to reassure him. "I can continue the village visits in peace. There are quite a few sick, but the abuses they endure need a remedy more than they do themselves; there is a great need for a permanent missionary here."

He pats his long white beard and begins to concentrate on organizing subsequent mission trips. It is the voice of the catechist which distracts him from his thoughts. It is evening now and time for Mass at the small church of the mission. Fr. Emilio hurries to the sacristy.

In Rome, on January 2, 1943, the Sacred Congregation for the Propagation of the Faith officially releases the news received in a telegram from Bishop Valtorta, announcing the death of Fr. Teruzzi: ."..killed, it seems, by Chinese brigands in the district of Cairn."

The first accounts of what happened are very vague. They lack the date, the place, and the details of the crime. Everything is based on a simple report, written in Latin, probably by a Chinese priest, and dated December 3, 1942:

> Eight days ago, Han Ah Kung (the sacristan of the church in Cairn) warned Fr. Teruzzi not to go visit the small villages, because the yiu-kit-du (guerrilla bands) considered him a traitor to China. Fr. Teruzzi responded that he is not a traitor, but simply concerned with caring for the souls of the Christians, and so he had

nothing to fear.

That same day, he went to visit Taitung, Tsengtau, and Wukaisa, saying that he would return in two days. He never came back. Yesterday evening, a Christian from the island, who does business in Cairn, told Ah Kung that Fr. Teruzzi had been killed. His body was then found and buried, but where, when, and how he did not know.

News received later from witnesses help to reconstruct what happened. Fr. Emilio was captured as he was preparing to celebrate the Eucharist in the house of some Christians. Taken out to sea, he was killed by a blow to the head with a rock, on November 26, 1942.

FR. VALERIANO FRACCARO

(MARCH 15, 1913 – SEPTEMBER 28, 1974)

It is a terrible blow to Fr. Francesco Frontini, the young 27-year-old missionary who finds the body. In Hong Kong only a few months, he has already become quite fond of Fr. Valeriano, just like anyone else who ever knew him.

"The evening of September 28, 1974," he recounts, "Father was alone in the house."

> We younger missionaries had hurried off right after dinner. I had to visit several mission chapels, and Fr. Adelio Lambertoni had been invited by some Chinese friends to celebrate the traditional Festival of the Moon. No one could have suspected what was to happen. At table, Fr. Valeriano had joked with the confreres and Chan Che-keung, his old friend and sacristan, and chatted with the three orphans adopted by the parish. Then the sacristan left and the orphans went to their rooms in a building not far away. Fr. Fraccaro was alone, but only in a manner of speaking. Whenever he is at the house there are always people coming and going: Christians, atheists, even Maoists. He was truly a friend of all. That evening, too, he had many visitors, up until ten or eleven o'clock.
>
> I came back at midnight and found him in his room. He was stripped, lying on the floor in a pool of blood, with a towel draped over his face. He had been

killed with an small axe, the type that is present in all
Chinese kitchens to cut meat.

But who could have killed him? Who could ever want to do him
harm? His white cassock, the rumpled bag that he always had with
him, the big umbrella he used as protection from the sun — all of
these were well known and loved in all thirty-seven villages of the district. The children always recognized him from afar by his distinctive
way of walking and ran shouting to meet him through the dusty roads,
which he always traveled on foot. He never had a car nor the desire to
learn how to drive. "Imagine, at my age!" he would laugh.

When he was younger, working in China, he used to go from one
place to another on an old beat-up bicycle, heavy as lead. The roads he
traveled were always filled with holes and stones. If it was raining, there
was no way to ride because of the thick mud, so he simply carried the
bike on his shoulders. He was unstoppable; it was impossible for him
to stay in one place for more than a couple of days. Even though the
bike was constantly in need of repair or replaced parts, he continued to
travel the length and breadth of southern Shensi diocese in the interior
of China.

In 1939, he wrote to his brother, Fr. Vittorino: "I am always
happy and in good health; my legs are still strong enough for the long
journeys, my room is peaceful and I sleep deeply, without dreams.
There is so much work here, it can take your breath away."

He had arrived with nothing in Hanzhong in 1937 at the age of
24. In fact, his luggage, sent from Italy by boat, was detained in a ware-
house because of the war. It was 1945 before he was able to get it out,
"… and by then, of course, I didn't need it," Fr. Valeriano recounted,
remembering those first years of the mission.

It was a difficult time. "The war continues, and we don't know
when it will end," he wrote in 1939.

The Japanese have begun bombing Hanzhong by air:
so many bombs, so much disaster and death. The last
time, more than thirty bombs were dropped on the

buildings of the vicariate. They bombed the seminary, the convent of the Canossian Sisters, the house of the catechist, the courtyard of the cathedral, the kitchen and bedrooms of the mission house. But why would the Japanese bomb our building when the bell tower has been painted with the three colors of Italy's flag? I still don't know. This should convince the Chinese that the Japanese are not our allies, much less our friends.

This is so much the case that when the occupying Japanese troops arrived, Fr. Valeriano was detained in a concentration camp. But that fact didn't help him much in 1949, when the communists controlled the area. Fr. Fraccaro was arrested again, and initially condemned to prison. But thanks to the kindness of the judge, the sentence was commuted to house arrest.

January, 1951:

> We are under the control of true masters. There is supposed to be freedom of religion, press and assembly, but they want to know all of our business, they claim that the police have a right to know everything, they forbid the Christians to go to church and prohibit the missionaries from carrying out our ministry. We are afraid that we will be sent out of China or imprisoned, but so far we have been able to stay at our posts. I'm preparing my baggage in case of expulsion. The church of Hanzhong, as is the case everywhere, is impoverished by enormous taxes. They are trying to turn us into beggars, to force us to ask the government for help, so that we will become their servants like everyone else. Last year I opened a dispensary at my house with two Chinese sisters to treat eye problems. But after a month and a half, I had to abandon everything, because we were taxed more than what we took in. The government is squeezing the church all over China, trying to close down its operations, to force out money

they believe is hidden, and so little by little to destroy the church.

Thus, in 1951, after many painful events, he was indeed expelled from China forever, branded as an enemy of the people. He managed to remain in Hong Kong, with the hope of one day returning to the "real China." Instead, it is in Hong Kong that he puts down roots.

The city swells each year, with 60 thousand newborns and almost 100 thousand refugees who flee communist China by any means, land or sea. Old people, women, children crowd the refugee camps at the borders, while others live on boats or in huts in the border districts: Kowloon, Lantao, Castle Peak, and Cairn. Fr. Valeriano travels a bit through all the districts, until in 1967 he is assigned to Cairn.

Untiring, he continues to visit all the villages and islands by carriage, by boat, on foot. "When I met Fr. Fraccaro," recalls an old Chinese woman, "I was still living in the distant village of Sa Chui."

I'll always remember the first time he came to the village. My house was in front of a small dock where the boats from Cairn would come every two days, so I could see the people who were arriving. That day I saw a short, pudgy man who, as soon as he got off the boat, opened his umbrella against the sun, and started with sure steps, almost running, toward the village. In a moment, he saw me at the door of my house. "Grandma," he called out to me, "I'm the new priest!" I liked the way he called me grandma (from that time on, it was the only way he addressed me), and his smile gave me confidence. I offered him tea and two fresh eggs, which he drank and ate immediately without ceremony.

He is not in Cairn very long when a violent typhoon hits and destroys everything. Fr. Valeriano organizes the relief work and seeks emergency shelter for the people. All the huts of the people have been inundated with mud except for those who live on their boats. The Chinese start to become familiar with his unlimited generosity.

"I met Fr. Valeriano in 1965, right after he arrived in Cairn," recalls a young teacher, who assisted Fr. Fraccaro for several years as a catechist, "because at that time I was attending the mission's high school."

> He was always smiling. He was funny looking, with his old fashioned glasses always sliding down his nose. The one thing that immediately attracted me to him was his beautiful smile. At the beginning, he seemed like a naive child, unaware of any problems; but living close to him I began to see his deep awareness of reality, and his ability to discuss things and get to the root of the matter. One indisputable fact is that he was loved by all: old people, children, teenagers. He knew how to adapt himself and live harmoniously with all types of people. He had a particular love for the old people, because he knew that they were the least cared for, the most lonely and needy. How many hours he spent visiting the old folks and talking with them, giving them the joy of a long chat!

His love for old people is so great that he even organizes the "Festival in Appreciation for the Aged." Coinciding with the Chinese New Year — when everyone goes into the city to celebrate, leaving the old folks at home alone — this feast invented by Fr. Valeriano is designed to give them some honor and dignity. He does everything himself: serves at table, sings, tells funny stories, and dispenses some good wine, a true luxury for the fishermen of Cairn; and there is always at least one old person who goes home a bit drunk. "What's wrong with that?" Fr. Valeriano would ask. "If it were evil, Our Lord would never have changed water into wine at the wedding in Cana."

He liked to joke, innocently, about the Gospel. "Today I was supposed to explain the parable of the Good Samaritan," he writes to his niece Paola in Castelfranco, "but I skipped it, telling my parishioners that this passage is too difficult. The truth is that in this parable, we priests don't come out looking very good, and so I said to myself, why should I speak badly about priests?" And he concludes ironically: "So what do you think of your uncle? Yet you know, Paola, that, after all, your uncle has a heart of gold, even if he makes *panettone* (an Italian cake) with stale flour and ants instead of raisins."

And *panettone* really has become his specialty! He mixes and bakes it himself, and pulls slices out of his rumpled bag, along with yellowing pictures of the saints, to give to the children. In fact, he comes to be known as the "baker priest." His relatives, who own a small bakery in Castelfranco Veneto, have sent him an old oven and he has fixed up a small hut where he makes bread and sweets. "They need it," he says, thinking of the skinny, malnourished children whose meals consist of a handful of seasoned rice and sometimes a little piece of fish. His breads with aromatic herbs are well known in the area, and they are eaten not only by the three thousand Christians of Cairn. Fr. Fraccaro has some for everybody: Catholics, Protestants, Buddhists, or Maoists. He works at night so that in the morning there is plenty of fresh bread to take around. He writes to his brothers in Italy to send a little sugar, so that he can also make sweets.

In all the homes, they love his "smiling face, streaming with sweat, which he wipes away with a large farmer's handkerchief." This earns him another nickname: "Pope John." For him, evangelization means personal relationships with the people, maintaining contact with all the families of the villages. He takes the boat at around 7:00 in the morning and returns at 10:00 or 11:00 at night. He visits the small dispersed villages, entering the huts to spend time with the sick, and joke with the old folks who can't move about. He finds the fishermen in their workplace, and celebrates the Mass wherever he happens to be, often on the boats where the fishermen live and sleep. He does this, he says, to create a community of faith and life. "When I say Mass there, I have to remain on my knees, because the roof is too low or the table is only a couple of feet high." But he enjoys himself there; he loves it among the Chinese, whom he understands perfectly: "They're like me, country people: big feet and sharp minds."

"He was very good to us," recalls a fisherman. "He never got angry at anyone, even though we fishermen are illiterate; if sometimes we used the wrong words in speaking, he used them too, to make us feel at home."

He is, then, a small "Pope John," with a smile born of evangelical simplicity, from a heart swollen with love, from a faith more powerful than the daily trials he must face. "As I see it, the world is beautiful," he writes to his sister-in-law, "even when there is difficulty and boredom, which simply strengthen us for life's experiences... I see my people, who are strong in faith, who don't give in to those who criticize or ridicule them: they really live what they believe..." And he is the first one to cultivate this deep relationship with God, in spite of a thousand duties and worries. "Even though we're busy with so many material things, we try to find a little time to gather before God and think about our souls." Thus, he manages to find some moments to spend in church, immersed in prayer, that prayer which is the source of so much peace and serenity for him.

"The thing that most impressed me about him," a Catholic girl of Cairn remembers, "was his dedication to help the needy. Anyone who came to him was certain to receive help. He went out in search of the poorest of the poor; he loved to help those that no one else was helping."

It is for this reason that he supports the initiative of his young confrere Fr. Lambertoni, to create the "Pope John Village," to offer a solid house on firm ground to the miserable people forced to live on their boats. The idea is simple. Pay the jobless men of the area to build brick houses, a school, even a small hospital; then rent these houses for a nominal amount (but enough to begin building new ones) to the needy families of boat people.

Indeed, by the 1970s poverty has reached gigantic proportions, and the bay has become more and more an unsanitary haven for refugees and the abandoned.

"It is more difficult now, to do missionary work and make conversions," he writes to his sister-in-law in 1972, "but it is also more consoling and appealing, I think."

The worldwide recession hits even this metropolis of rampant capitalism. The small factories which make plastic sandals, toys and electronic gadgets, which survive only through exportation, close one after another. Meanwhile, the city is simmering; the influx of refugees is constant and aggravates the problem of unemployment. With the poverty, crime begins to spread like a stain of oil. Teenage gangs attack, loot, and destroy sometimes out of need and sometimes just to be rowdy. The violence, at first confined to the city, is now expanding to the outlying districts, including Cairn. This little fishing village is under the constant threat of gangs which rob, blackmail, commit revenge killings and other crimes. Fr. Fraccaro suffers in this situation; when he speaks of it, he loses his smile. Yet, he never ceases to invest his energy and his optimism to help "his people." He continues to work, and even though he is himself as poor as the people he serves, he never refuses anything to anyone who asks. Everyone loves him. Who could ever want to do him harm?

But on September 28, 1974, an evening like any other, he is killed in his own home by someone who came in through the kitchen door, always left open for those who wanted to find a good word or a hot loaf of bread. An unknown killer. Maybe he was sent by one who was hoping to develop luxury homes on the beach, where the missionary had built houses for the poor.

BURMA:
LAND OF MYSTERY
AND INTRIGUE

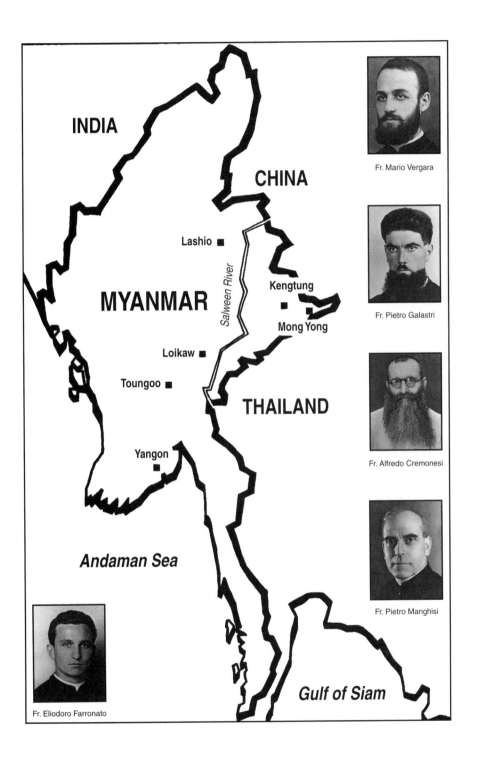

INDIA

CHINA

Lashio ■

Salween River

MYANMAR

Kengtung

■

Mong Yong

Loikaw ■

Toungoo ■

THAILAND

Yangon

■

Andaman Sea

Gulf of Siam

Fr. Mario Vergara

Fr. Pietro Galastri

Fr. Alfredo Cremonesi

Fr. Pietro Manghisi

Fr. Eliodoro Farronato

INTRODUCTION

By Fr. Piero Gheddo

THERE ARE REALLY TWO BURMAS. ONE IS VISITED BY WESTERNERS ON trips organized by a travel agency: Rangoon, Pegu, Bessein, Taunggyi, Mandalay, Pagan. In seven packed days you can see great monuments such as the Shwedagon Pagoda in the capital and the ruins of Pagan, the most fascinating "ghost town" in the world (Pompeii pales by comparison). But there is also a second Burma, much more authentic, which the tourists do not see: villages of raised wooden huts with straw roofs, in which live some of the poorest and most repressed people of the world. A potentially rich country, Burma is more than twice the size of California with only 43 million inhabitants.

I've visited the country twice, and I focused my attention especially on the "second" Burma — the mountains and forests — where tribal peoples live in the midst of war, disease, and famine. These areas were first evangelized by P.I.M.E. missionaries, who founded five dioceses: Toungoo, Kengtung, Taunggyi, Lashio, and Loikaw. All of them now have indigenous clergy. Along with six Sisters of the Child Jesus, there are only seven Italian missionaries left, including the Bishop Emeritus of Taunggyi, Giovanni Battista Gobbato.

Before British colonization, Burma was known as the Kingdom of Ava and Pegu (the two capitals). A strong military force dominated the region, including Siam (present-27

day Thailand). In 1826 and 1852, the British occupied some provinces of this kingdom and declared southern Burma a province of the British Empire.

In two more colonial wars in 1884 and 1886, the British conquered all of Burma and considered it a part of the Anglo-Indian empire. The country saw great development in the lowlands (the Valley of Irrawaddy), mostly inhabited by ethnic Burmese (Buddhists), while the mountains and forests of the tribal minorities (animists) were virtually ignored by the colonizers. This deepened the stark division between the dominant race and the ethnic minorities, who had already been oppressed by the Burmese in the past.

In 1941, Burma was invaded by the Japanese, who entered from the north, from China, which they had already conquered. In 1945 the Burmese rebelled against the Japanese and in 1948, they declared independence from Great Britain. Immediately, separatist movements began among the various tribes. These rebellions would gain momentum due to the oppression wreaked throughout the whole country by the Burmese military, which took over the government in a coup on March 2, 1962 and continues to hold power even today. In addition, in the area bordering Thailand, Laos, and China (the so-called "Golden Triangle," from which comes more than 50 percent of the drugs exported to the West), opium is cultivated and marketed. Thus, mixed in with the guerrilla bands who are inspired by a spirit of patriotic independence (Karen, Lahu, Shan, Wa, etc.) are drug traffickers, brigands, branches of the Chinese-Burmese Communist Party, and the remnants of the armed nationalists of Chiang Kai-shek. The latter fled China in 1949 and established themselves along the Burmese border, where for 45 years they have survived on illegal commerce and banditry.

P.I.M.E. has worked in Burma since 1868, and the story of opening the northeast regions of the country (the very Golden Triangle mentioned above) to the Gospel is one of the most adventurous and glorious in the Institute's history. The five martyrs remembered in this chapter were killed here. They are certainly true martyrs because it was their faithfulness to their missionary vocation and love for their people that brought them to such a dangerous place, at the risk of their own lives. Two were killed in 1950, Mario Vergara and Pietro Galastri; two in 1953, Pietro Manghisi and Alfredo Cremonesi; one in 1955, Eliodoro Farronato. But along with them, many other Christians were killed, including indigenous priests and sisters such as Fr. Stefano Vong, the first native priest of the diocese of Kengtung, killed on April 10, 1961.

In order to understand the martyrdom of these missionaries, of Fr. Vong and so many other Catholics, it is necessary to remember that war has been going on in Burma for 45 years, "the longest war in the world," the war of liberation waged by the tribal minorities against the government of Rangoon. Of the 43 million inhabitants of Burma 72 percent are ethnic Burmese, while the other 28 percent is made up of the tribes who live in the "second" Burma, which Western tourists are never allowed to visit: Shan (9 percent), Mon (4 percent), Karen (2.5 percent), Kachin (2.2 percent), Padaung, Lahu, Musho, Akhà, Wa, Lisho, Ikò, etc. Such a multitude of peoples, separated by language and traditions, are all united in the rejection of Burmese dominance.

Burma, which at one time was the richest country in south Asia, has become the poorest and most oppressed after the military takeover in 1962 and the installation of a "socialist" dictatorship. The regime, like all socialist elites, has blocked all economic and social development, and survives by oppressing the people with continual violations of human rights.

This tragic situation afflicts, most of all, the tribal peoples who live in these regions, the very regions evangelized by the P.I.M.E. Missionaries. The ethnic Burmese are Buddhists, who rarely convert to Christianity. The tribals practice animism (based on the belief in and cult of the spirits) and are open to the preaching of the Gospel.

The martyrdom of the five P.I.M.E. missionaries and so many of their Christians has its origin in the guerrilla warfare and chaos of northeast Burma, where rebel bands, military deserters, brigands, and the private armies of the drug traffickers abound. The national Burmese army, whose duty it is to establish order and protect the people, acts more like an occupying force in the tribal areas, killing, burning, and looting villages, using every kind of violence against the common people.

The missionaries and the Christian communities, who stand for peace and reconciliation and do not accept violence as a common rule of behavior, are the ones who suffer the most severe consequences of the war.

FR. MARIO VERGARA

(NOVEMBER 16, 1910 – MAY 24, 1950)

About eight kilometers north of Naples, Italy is the industrial town of Frattamaggiore, famous for the production of hemp. The many factories offer good opportunities for employment for the people of the region. It is 1910. One of these factories is managed by Gennaro Vergara (also an alderman of the town), who often travels to foreign countries, especially Germany, where most of his products are exported. While he is away, his wife Antonietta takes over his duties in the factory. She handles all of the administration without neglecting her home and her nine children.

The youngest of five brothers is Mario, born that year on November 16.

"He was an adventurous, fun-loving lad," recalls his boyhood companion and great friend Gennaro Auletta:

> After elementary school, in 1921, he entered the diocesan seminary of Aversa. The superiors there probably didn't have much hope for him. His open and carefree attitude was seen more as rebelliousness. Certainly, those who never really got close to him or came to know him well could consider him rather brusque. But a great heart was always beating under that rough exterior.

Indeed, inspired by a great love for God and each member of the human family, he endures the discipline of the seminary and grows very strong in his vocation. In October of 1929, Mario enters the

P.I.M.E. seminary in Monza. But before the end of the school year, he has to return home because of a severe attack of appendicitis, followed quickly by life-threatening peritonitis. But Mario is sure of his destiny, so much so that he would later remember: "All around me people were crying, but I just smiled to myself. I knew I couldn't die, because I had to become a missionary!" And sure enough, he recovers.

To protect his still feeble health from the harsh northern winters, Mario continues his studies at the Pontifical Seminary in Campano di Posillipo, run by the Jesuits; while there he gets very involved in promoting missionary awareness.

In August of 1933, he is able to reenter P.I.M.E., and with much gratitude he writes to the superior: "The joy which fills my heart is so great that it is impossible to put into words my feelings of thankfulness for the wonderful gift you have given me."

In Milan he completes his last year of theology and on August 24, 1934, he is ordained a priest. His friend Gennaro recalls: "He was so moved by his ordination that at the party in his honor given by the seminarians of Frattamaggiore, he hardly said a word. He couldn't even smile for the group photo!"

A month later he leaves for Burma.

As soon as he arrives in Toungoo, at the end of October, 1934, Fr. Vergara throws himself into the study of the languages spoken by the Karen tribes. After a few months, when he is relatively fluent in three of them, he is assigned to the district of Citaciò, inhabited by the Sokùs. There are 29 Catholic villages to attend to, catechists to train, and 50 orphans to care for.

"Everyone held him in great esteem, including the indigenous clergy," recalls his confrere Fr. Mora:

> Beneath a rather gruff attitude was a heart of gold. When you first meet him, you might be put off, but if you get to know him, you quickly discover a man of exquisite tenderness. He was famous, in fact, for his love for children and the sick. He had an almost maternal attitude toward the sick children of the orphanage,

tending them day and night, bathing them and giving them medicine.

Fr. Mario is always on the move. Undeterred by discomforts, bad weather, the malaria which frequently attacks him, he goes out to visit the villages, sometimes even in the grip of a fever. He takes on dozens of roles for his people: priest, educator, doctor, administrator, and often even judge.

Then, suddenly, the war interrupts his dreams and activities. On June 10, 1940, Italy declares war on England. The Italian missionaries are considered "fascists" and automatically become enemies of the British.

Fr. Mario must withdraw to the P.I.M.E. house of formation in Momblo. Here he concentrates on the study of yet another local language, Ghekù, in the vain hope of being able to communicate with this tribal people. But soon the Japanese also enter the scene; after the attack on Pearl Harbor, they quickly invade the Philippines, Indochina, Hong Kong, and Thailand. Now they are on the doorstep of Burma.

The Catholic missionaries not already interned by the British stay put in their backwoods missions and try to hold on through the many dangers and ordeals. However, when the Japanese invade Burmese territory on December 21, 1941, all of the Italians, including Fr. Vergara, are sent to concentration camps in India.

The missionaries are among the civilian prisoners of war and their biggest burden is simply inactivity. Life in the concentration camp is extremely boring. "The memory of my mission drives me crazy, as I stand here behind barbed wire with nothing to do," writes Fr. Grazioso Banfi from the Bombay internment camp on January 25, 1943.

> When I think of the work there is to be done, tears
> come to my eyes. Meanwhile, I pray, suffer, and study
> for my mission. Almost all the P.I.M.E. missionaries
> (82 by now) have been here for two years... The days
> don't pass as quickly as we'd like. But when will peace
> come? Our poor missions! The Lord, if He has

deemed to allow this, will find some way to bring good out of it.

And with this confidence they go on. Meanwhile, after the inspection of the Red Cross, and the insistence of the Vatican and the Catholic Bishops of India, on March 15, 1943, the Italian civilian detainees are transferred to a wing of the camp where conditions are a bit better. The missionaries, grouped in two nearby barracks, can take greater care of their spiritual life and their studies.

In hope of returning to Burma, they study the Karen languages, they organize theological seminars and courses in medicine; they discuss their different pastoral styles; they hold conferences on liturgy and morals; they reflect upon the constitution of the Institute. The days are not quite so unendingly bleak and boring anymore. They are even able to build a little chapel for perpetual adoration. Even though it seems like the captivity will never end, thanks to the hope that they radiate, the missionaries are able to give comfort to all of those living under the same conditions.

Around the end of 1944, the first fathers are released and can return to their missions.

After four years of difficult and unnerving captivity, Fr. Mario Vergara is also released. He is very weak because, in addition to the general exhaustion brought on by the harsh detention, he immediately undergoes several surgeries, one of which results in the removal of a kidney. He is afraid that he will now be considered useless and worried that he might be sent home for a rest, or even for good. But this is not the case; instead, he is very soon given a most arduous and dangerous assignment.

Bishop Lanfranconi has in mind to establish a mission center at the extreme eastern border of the mission of Toungoo among a new tribe of people. There is, therefore, a new language to learn, as well as new customs and traditions. The area consists of one hundred villages spread throughout the jungle. It seems like an impossible plan. He speaks about it with Fr. Mario who, without hesitation, accepts the challenge.

The new district is located over six thousand feet high in the Prèt-hole mountain chain, a two-day trip east of Loikaw. It consists of many villages with traditional religions and a few Baptist villages. In 1939, two villages became Catholic, but then with the war, everything came to a halt. The people of these two villages welcome Fr. Vergara with festivities on December 26, 1946.

He begins with nothing. There is not even a hole or a cave for him to live in, not a mat to lie upon. Fr. Mario does what he can with an abandoned hut.

> I now live in a bamboo hut on the top of a mountain near the village of Tarudà [one of the two Catholic villages he found when he arrived]. Wind and sun enter freely; when it rains, I have an indoor bath, just like the rich folks. Hey, when you're born under a lucky star...! As for furniture, I have two chairs and a little table, which I made with my catechist's machete; for food, there's a little rice with forest herbs. To the left, the mountain chain sweeps down to the lowland of Loikaw. It's a well populated area; there are two hundred villages of red Karen and a few of Shan. The Protestants arrived here twenty years ago, and they have four villages. Very soon, I will make a trip to get acquainted with the area, together with a Karen priest and some catechists.

With his typical enthusiasm, calm, measured, and firm, he confronts his new life. Surely it can't be easy, so far away from the mission center, amid such poverty, with no provisions and no means of transportation. More difficult than the material discomforts is the effort to fit in and to dialogue with the people, with the Buddhists, and even more, with the Baptists. But all these obstacles do nothing to blunt the eagerness of Fr. Vergara who begins passionately to study the local language, so that he can make contact with the villages and begin to train catechists.

His medical knowledge comes in quite handy. Sometimes it

seems that he can perform "miracles": an unconscious baby recovers thanks to a sip of Mass wine, which Fr. Mario gives him because he has no medicine with him; a cripple, who limps along painfully, is able to get up and walk after his muscles are massaged. These two extraordinary recoveries arouse the suspicions of the Baptists who, fearing the "competition," begin to spread rumors about him. "While I am looking for some teachers," he recounts, "some Protestants arrive and begin speaking ill of our religion. The people, disgusted, accept neither me nor them. This is a terrible suffering. Only the prayers of those who love me can sustain me."

In October of 1948, some help arrives in the person of Fr. Pietro Galastri, and he is just the assistant needed. With him, a good carpenter and mason, they can finally think about building a church, a school, an orphanage, and a dispensary. Together, then, the two fathers settle in the large market area of Shadow, populated by Shan Buddhists, and begin their construction projects. Fr. Mario, meanwhile, helped and encouraged by the presence of his confrere, continues his efforts as a "wandering apostle" among the mountains and rice fields.

His greatest desire is to train catechists so that his own European faith can be translated into the local culture and Christianity can thus become understandable and convincing. But this is a difficult task, and he must constantly deal with the traditions and superstitions of the area. As if this were not enough, many try to take advantage of these simple people. One charlatan, for example, pretending to be a prophet, promises money, rice, well-being and above all, immortality. Just believe in his god and make a lot of offerings. Meanwhile, the fields go uncultivated, the villages are abandoned and families disintegrate. Obviously, the illusion doesn't last long, and it is up to Fr. Vergara to help these people face the resulting misery, which has become even more squalid, and the moral degradation. To this end, he institutes an activity similar to Catholic Action.

With his pastoral activities, Fr. Vergara incurs the ill-will of the Protestants, lately grown worse because of the new political situation following independence of the country from England in 1948. Fr. Mario writes:

When the British were in control, there was order and peace; now, there is chaos and civil war. The Protestant Karens, taking advantage of the general confusion, have taken power in some areas and terrorize the Catholics who are faithful to the legitimate government.

Fr. Gerolamo Clerici adds in a 1949 article:

In January of 1949, Toungoo is occupied by the Karen rebels. But after some initial success, this ragtag army begins to feel the effects of the government's counterattack and is in danger of defeat on every front. The rebel chieftain, in order to feed his hungry troops, steals provisions and imposes heavy taxes on the people of the important market town of Shadow.

Fr. Vergara cannot remain silent in the face of this oppression and rises to the defense of his people. His intervention wins him the gratitude of the village chief, but only intensifies the hatred of the rebels, especially their leader, Tire, who already dislikes Fr. Mario because of his religious "successes."

In January of 1950, the position of Fr. Vergara and his assistant Fr. Galastri worsens when Loikaw, the only place where provisions can be obtained, falls under the control of the government troops. Their mission is now cut in two by the opposing forces, and the fathers often must cross the lines to go from their residence in Shadow to the villages which have been retaken by the government.

At the end of the month, returning to Shadow from Loikaw, Frs. Mario and Pietro are stopped and searched by the rebels, who hope to find them in possession of arms or compromising documents. The result of the search is negative, but this does nothing to allay the suspicions that the missionaries are spies of the central government.

Meanwhile, in Loikaw, months pass without any news of Frs. Vergara and Galastri, and the bishop and confreres are worried about their fate. Finally, on August 31, 1950 it is announced on local radio that the two missionaries have been arrested and killed, their bodies thrown into the Salween river.

Only later do more details arrive. On May 24, at six o'clock in the morning, some rebels enter the mission residence in Shadow, where Fr. Galastri is at prayer, and order him to follow them. Bound hand and foot, he is taken to the marketplace where, in the meantime, Fr. Vergara has also been brought, along with the catechist Isidoro, both having been arrested in the village square. At nightfall all three are made to walk along the left bank of the Salween river, and at dawn of the twenty-fifth, they are killed by rifle shots. Their bodies, tied up in sacks, are cast into the flowing river.

FR. PIETRO GALASTRI

(APRIL 18, 1918 – MAY 24, 1950)

The siren sounds, and the ship moves away from port. We gather on the bridge, take up the accordion and begin to sing. We sing with all our heart and soul: hymns to the Virgin Mary, sending prayers to the Queen of Heaven that she will help us in this final farewell, that she will bless those who leave and those who are united with us in prayer at this moment.

Genoa disappears little by little. Genoa, wonderful Genoa, slips away from us. Her lights, always so beautiful and lively, slowly begin to fade. The stars and the moon join our chorus, which slowly begins to soften. The tormented voice of the wind drowns out the song, until it dies in the sad silence of the night; dies in the infinite solitude, dies on the waves of the sea, upon which our ship, with its monotonous noise, echoes our voices. And finally only the ship itself continues the song, leaving behind a long wake, which takes the shape of a rope, still uniting us with our homeland.

The cool air, the weariness, the sadness urge us to sleep. Everyone leaves the bridge to take their rest. I remain alone, leaning on the rail; with a melancholy gaze, I keep watching that wake and those distant lights.

It's 10:00 p.m. I pray and think, think and pray, for everyone. Sadness invades my spirit; I walk along the deck, praying the rosary. My thoughts return to my family home, where every evening we would gather in front of Our Lady of Sorrows, to recite the rosary, led by my father.

It's Tuesday, the day when the prospective candidates to the seminary gather for their meeting. I feel like I'm there in the auditorium with them, looking once again at the lively faces of those young men; it seems like they are responding, as always, to the Hail Marys of the rosary. As I finish my prayer, the dream ends as well, and I return to reality: I'm on a ship, cutting through the waves; and beyond the horizon, Genoa disappears completely.

Father Pietro Galastri writes the above, in the first pages of his travel diary. It is March 23, 1948, and he is leaving Italy on the steamer *Taurinia*, heading for Burma.

He is tall, straight, severe, with marked features; deep, penetrating, lively eyes and a full black beard on his long, austere face. In spite of his imposing looks, his heart is filled with strong passions and great dreams. He is thirty years old, and finally, after five years of forced waiting, he is able to leave, to go toward the goal for which he has been yearning for so long.

Born on April 18, 1918, at the age of thirteen he communicates to the rector of the missionary seminary of Agazzi his desire to "become a priest." His cousin, Cesare Mencattini, is already in the seminary, and Pietro, who has visited him often, nourishes the same dream.

Thus, from Partina, a small village in the Camaldoli mountains, Pietro Galastri goes to Agazzi (Arezzo), leaving behind his parents and eight brothers, the dense forest of beech and firs, the green valley, the quiet of the monastery and cloister of Camaldoli.

Before World War II, there was a small minor seminary for the foreign missions in Agazzi, an isolated village surrounded by open fields, about five kilometers from Arezzo. The first year of this new life is not easy for Pietro. Used to independence, taken up with school, household chores, games, and outdoor pastimes, the change in lifestyle is quite abrupt for him: strict discipline, rigid rules, a difficult and monotonous schedule. Soon he adapts, but as the years continue, he transfers to other seminaries of the Institute in the province of Caserta, first in Ducenta and then in Aversa. Now besides the discipline of the seminary, he has to face the first true separation from his family. Agazzi was close to his home, and it was easy for his family to visit him; now the distance is greater. This separation does not diminish his affection for his family, however, and in fact his brothers find the time to come and visit him whenever they can.

Neither is his enthusiasm for the choice he has made diminished in the least; rather, it is more clearly defined, reinforced, and enriched. For example, upon return from the war in east Africa, his brother passes through Ducenta, where Pietro is attending his sixth year of seminary. "He wanted me to stay even longer than usual," writes Luigi, "so that he could ask me questions about the life of the 'natives.'"

> He wanted to know what is going on in the other parts of our church. His questions were full of anxiety and enthusiasm. He dreamed that soon he would come to know those creatures so different from us, with whom I had been in brutal combat. He wanted to embrace them and bring them to the Lord. His words, he said, would be more effective than my gun, because they were the fruit of love and conviction!

In the spring of 1937, Pietro transfers to the P.I.M.E. seminary in Monza. Besides facing the struggles of schoolwork, he has to endure the beginning of World War II and the English bombings. The danger becomes so great that in 1943, the theology courses are moved to Villa Grugana in Brianza, where Galastri can continue his studies. On December 18, 1943, he is ordained a priest. He is ready to be sent to the missions right away, but the war is still going on, and the borders are closed. He and his classmates can do nothing but wait.

In the meantime, they are given the chance to exercise their priestly ministry in the parishes of Lombardy. This pastoral work is beneficial in two ways: it provides experience which will be useful in the missions and at the same time gives much needed help to the diocese. Many young diocesan priests have gone to serve as military chaplains, leaving the pastors alone in the parishes. Thus, on September 9, 1944, Fr. Galastri is assigned as assistant pastor in Groppello, a village of Cassano d'Adda, in the province of Milan. Young, active, determined, and full of enthusiasm, Giovanni dives into the apostolic work with all of his energy. He is particularly dedicated to the youth, organizing activities which are fun and educational at the same time: plays which are put on in neighboring villages, unforgettable trips, moments of intense joy and communion, delight at the arrival of the first movie projector in the area. He engages intimately in parish life and the life of his parishioners, he tends the orphans at the Piccola Opera Tognoli, he fixes an old sewing machine and finds a young woman to teach the children how to use it.

At the end of 1947, he receives the news that he will soon leave for the missions. The insistent pleas of the people of Groppello that the "bearded father" forgo his departure and remain with them fall on deaf ears. On March 23, 1948 he sails for Burma.

After about a month and a half, the ship reaches Calcutta on May 4 and will not leave for Rangoon until the twelfth; but his visa expires on the ninth. He must take an airplane in order to be out of the country in time.

> From above, the immense Ganges with all its tributaries looks like a gigantic spiderweb. And now the turbulence begins! Buckle up well! For hundreds of meters we are falling into the void, and we instinctively try to stand up; we are wide-eyed, breathless, with hearts pounding. Then the plane goes roaring up again. A nervous laugh and everything is okay but soon enough it starts all over again, even more frightening than before. Finally the sky clears, the sun returns, and we regain our balance.

There it is! Dear Burma, so long awaited, I salute you! How beautiful you are! Mountains, forests, valleys, villages, and immense plains. Rangoon, the capital, hurries to meet us. Here is the airport: one bump, two, three, the wheels turn on the iron runway. We stop. We get off the plane. In three and a quarter hours, we have come 1200 kilometers!

The next morning, May 8, we leave by train for Toungoo; in seats built in the Burmese style, we have to cross our legs and sit on our heels. The railway stations are raised huts. Only the pagodas, which dominate here, are made of brick. Oh Lord, your Kingdom come! At Toungoo Bishop Alfredo Lanfranconi is waiting for us. After a brief *Te Deum* in the wooden cathedral, we begin our missionary life. Here we must live in huts, sleep on mats, and do our best to eat rice and more rice. The joy of the missionaries is something incredible! I have never seen men more filled with happiness than these veterans!

In the first months, it is a great penance for Fr. Pietro not to be able to speak with the children. The most pressing need is to study the local languages. Meanwhile, the bishop notes that Fr. Galastri is a clever and tireless worker. He could be a precious co-worker of Fr. Vergara in Prèthole, where there is so much to do, and besides he would have a chance to practice the language with the people there. Thus, he is assigned to the most difficult and distant post.

"A look of pure joy lit up my face. I'm leaving for my assignment!" He goes by train, by truck, on horseback, and on foot. Yet these discomforts are nothing compared to the conditions of anarchy and chaos now beginning to afflict all of Burma. The government is weak and ineffective; the opposing forces take the opportunity to attack it. Communist guerrillas come in from China: they assault and burn villages, steal, destroy, murder. Add to all this the Baptists, who oppose the Catholics. The people fear the rebels and do not feel safe to go into their fields to plant rice. News arrives of burned-out villages, whole communities exterminated, crops destroyed. The few government soldiers seem powerless to do anything.

Missionary work also becomes impossible. Railroad lines are blown up; truck service is hampered by the guerrillas hiding in the forest and along the roads. There is not one corner of this great country which enjoys peace and security. Meanwhile, almost on the day Fr. Galastri arrives, the government decides that no new missionaries will be allowed to enter. "I got here just in time! A week later and I would not have been able to enter Burma. The missionaries who are here can stay, but new ones are not permitted to come in."

It is in this situation, in Taruddà, a Catholic village deep in the jungle, amid "dilapidated huts," that Fr. Pietro begins his work, together with Fr. Vergara. "It seems crazy! But here I am, and I must dance! And so — we dance for the glory of God!"

In his two years in Burma, he undertakes enormous work. He constructs buildings of wood and brick, equips rooms for catechesis and other pastoral activities, all without neglecting his apostolic duties, teaching, and preaching. With Fr. Mario he tends to the instruction of the children and provides food for the orphans.

After building a small wooden church in Taruddà, the two fathers move their headquarters to Shadow. There they need to build and care for the residence, the church, a school, an orphanage, and a dispensary.

> From 7:00 a.m. to 2:00 p.m., I greet the people who come from the mountains to the market of Shadow. Some simply pass by, some stay for a while to observe us, to seek counsel, to ask for medicine. The teacher, Isidoro, translates for me and we try to help everyone. But it takes a lot of patience.

And in the afternoon, he is architect, carpenter, and builder. "When the Karens watch me work, they ask for whatever medicine I'm taking, so that they can become strong like me. And yet, I'm so skinny!"

Soon, however, the troubles begin. When Loikaw is occupied by the rebels, Fr. Pietro writes: "Here in Shadow we are cut off from our source of provisions, Loikaw, because no one wants to go there. Thus, we have to impose rationing on everything. Pray for me; since I don't know the language well, I suffer most of all."

Beginning in July of 1949, communication becomes increasingly difficult. In Italy, they wait in vain for some news. Fr. Galastri is holed up in Shadow, where he oversees the construction of the church and school. From Loikaw, the bishop and Fr. Vergara assure his friends that he is fine, but there is an "iron curtain" and he cannot move from there. Finally, in September, he is able to join his confreres. "Life is difficult," he writes in response to the letters from Italy, "but in God's name we carry on!"

> How do I pass the time? In work, disillusionment and privation... I fight on with my tongue between my teeth and my gaze fixed on God. Did you think I was dead and buried? No, I'm alive and healthy; in fact, very healthy, robust and strong. Fr. Vergara, on the other hand, suffers from chronic malaria. May God preserve him! To work all day and keep watch all night is not so bad. But to be alone! No, please not that! I've had some adventures, but always ended up fine, with even more strength and courage, which come as gifts of God in answer to your prayers. I am happy, even when my heart is bleeding! I am never tempted to regret having come here! Oh my dear friends, in the midst of sadness, trials and privations of every kind, we always feel happy here, even blessed. If there is a moment of hesitation, with a glance at heaven we once again feel strong and ready for anything!

As time passes, the guerrilla warfare intensifies.

One day, an armed band breaks into the hut of Fr. Galastri, while he is at prayer. His children are there with him. The bandits accuse him of hiding arms and being a spy of the government army. Their search turns up nothing, but still they take him away, and force him to walk toward the jungle with his hands behind his head, threatening to kill him. This is only a warning, the first inkling of what would happen later. He himself gives news of these events, writing that "God has arranged things in this way for the good of the mission."

With great faith he faces death every day. And when that distant area of Prèthole also falls into the hands of the rebels, Fr. Pietro, a calm and quiet man, always at the side of his confrere, shares his fate. It is May 25, 1950.

FR. ALFREDO CREMONESI

(MAY 15, 1902 – FEBRUARY 7, 1953)

February 20, 1946; Toungoo, Burma:

It's been six years now of forced silence. The war has been terribly long and the trial for us more difficult than I can describe. For four years it was a colonial war, and that is the worst kind, because everyone is more interested in stealing than anything else. I had to escape into the jungle, and I assure you, during the rainy season that's not a pleasant place to be, especially when you have nothing. I had only the clothes on my back. There was no oil for cooking; bread was unheard of. For years we went without sugar, and sometimes there wasn't even any salt. We used anything we could for clothes, and wore wooden clogs for shoes. All the markets were looted and empty; there was no such thing as a shop. All the means of communication were taken over by the Japanese for their war effort. The roads were battered and destroyed by the constant bombing of the British. Exchange of goods from region to region was absolutely impossible.

Yes, we have suffered terribly, and it's no wonder that now I'm very tired. But it is a weariness which can be overcome. I'm alive. This is a great grace, after having to face death every day. Clearly, the Lord has protected me.

Fr. Alfredo Cremonesi has already been in the mission of Burma for 20 years when he writes this letter, having faced all kinds of sufferings, including the effects of the Second World War, as he describes here. Who would have thought that he would be able to endure such physical distress, when ever since his youth he suffered from weak health, so much so that he was in danger of death more than once?

Years earlier, no one would have bet on his success in becoming a missionary. Afflicted with a lymph disorder and a blood disease, he had to spend long periods in bed during his high-school years at the diocesan seminary of Crema, without any hope of a cure. Dozens of treatments had proved ineffective; the doctors and his family were beginning to believe that the end was near. And even when it was clear that he would live, it was also evident that he would always be sickly, always in need of medicine and extra vitamins.

Instead, he was completely cured. He had been sure that this would be the case. He had entrusted himself to St. Therese of the Child Jesus, and he knew that she would grant him this special grace. Thus, once recovered, he decides to transfer from the diocesan seminary and become a missionary.

The obstacles are not completely overcome, however. Now he has to deal with his family. Indeed, his father, while a deeply committed Christian, very much involved with Catholic Action, absolutely opposes Alfredo's decision. But Alfredo does not give up, and with the help of his mother, he receives his father's blessing to attend the Seminary for Foreign Missions in Milan, entering the third year of theology in October of 1922, at the age of twenty.

Always on the go, impetuous in word and deed, he enthusiastically jumps into every new activity. He loves to write short stories and poetry and many Catholic publications print his articles. He is a brilliant writer, and ends up teaching Italian to the high-school students while he is finishing up his theological studies.

On October 12, 1924, he is ordained a priest and exactly one year later he leaves for Burma.

Alfredo is only 23 years old when he sails from Genoa toward that unknown land, yet he bravely bids goodbye to his parents, younger brothers and friends, knowing that he would never again return to his homeland.

Arriving in Toungoo on November 10, 1925, Fr. Alfredo finds himself in a world completely different from his own. For a year he must dedicate himself to studying the language and culture, after which he is assigned as treasurer of the mission. He handles the accounts, prepares the budgets, sends necessary items for the schools, churches, orphanages, and dispensaries of the missionaries who are far off in their districts. He's not sure this is what he expected out of missionary life, but he attends to his duties, all the while dreaming of something else:

> Standing here in Toungoo, I gaze out at the mountain chain, which rises like smoke on the distant horizon. It is the region of western Yoma, where there are many Karen tribes. How I wish to be in that mountainous area…

Soon his dream is realized. The bishop assigns him to a new district and Donoku, an isolated mountain village, becomes his point of departure for many missionary journeys. Thus he begins his "gypsy life, traveling among Catholic and pagan villages," becoming one of the more tireless travelers among his confreres.

Indeed, as he himself writes:

> The villages are generally quite distant from one another, because these mountains are mostly reserved for the cultivation of the precious teak trees, a real financial bonanza for the government. There is an army of those assigned to watch the plants, to count their years and months. The villages, then, are restricted to certain areas, and you can sometimes walk a full day without seeing anyone. That means you need to carry everything with you, if you don't want to die of hunger.

His enthusiasm is great, but his youthful inexperience and impatience soon bring him face to face with his own fragility and humanity:

I'll tell you the truth: many times I find myself crying like a baby at the thought of how much there is to be done and my absolute lack of ability. More than once, laden down by the weight of discouragement, I have asked the Lord if it wouldn't better for me to die than to be such an ineffective worker.

Yet, it is precisely in this deep, intimate union with God, that he finds the strength to continue.

In fact, to a great extent, he lives his missionary vocation in prayer. He dedicates a lot of time to adoration and does not hesitate to spend many hours of the night in front of the Eucharist. This is his anchor, his salvation, especially in the most difficult moments of solitude.

After ten years in the mountains, he writes:

What does it mean for me to be alone? It means so many things that if I were to begin to list them for you, I would never finish. It means a ton of hardships, which I should be used to by now, but which instead continue to wear me down more and more. My poor legs have a hard time climbing these mountain trails. In a week of travels, I pass through an extraordinary variety of illnesses, and I'm always amazed to be still on my feet when I get back home. And I'm only 35 years old. It's a shame, isn't it, to be so weak at this age? Maybe it's due to the climate, maybe the food, maybe so many worries; but most of all it's due to my constant poverty, which makes me continually add another hole to my belt and convince myself that the many things I do without are useless anyway.

All of this brings him to a maturity of faith and a profound awareness that he himself is but a useless instrument in the hands of God.

We missionaries are really nothing. Ours is the most mysterious and marvelous work ever given a person, not to perform, but to see happening: to discover souls who are converted is a miracle greater than any other.

This is the power which enables him to continue, in spite of everything.

> The light will always penetrate, little by little, even the densest fog; and a missionary never works in vain, even in the most sterile fields. I am more certain of this now than ever.
>
> As a beginner, I took all such difficulties too seriously and was thrown into discouragement. Often I was on the verge of giving up everything and seeking refuge in one of the more established missions. But who can resist the burning zeal which has made us missionaries and sent us into these savage lands? The fire is inside, and it is demanding. So now I continue my work, and when I least expect it, I see some fruits. The Spirit blows where he will and I continue to be a witness to him.

Thus he carries on his apostolic journeys, allowing himself to be forged by God, who is acting not only outside of him, but inside as well. Indeed, even in the midst of his personal crises, he is always ready to serve, always happy. His interior joy and serenity radiate forth from him so much that the people of the villages come to refer to him as "the smile of the mission."

In 1941, World War II is coming closer to Burma every day. Upon the arrival of the Japanese on Burmese soil, the English intern the missionaries in concentration camps in India, except for six veterans who have been in their place for more than ten years. Among these is Fr. Cremonesi, who remains at Mosò until the end of the war.

Even more lonely and deprived of everything, he must confront tribulations of every sort. He is forced to eat grass cooked in water and salt. Already reduced to a skeleton and exhausted by malnourishment, he is attacked by malarial fever.

But even greater than the physical privations are the moral sufferings. Up until 1943, the Italian missionaries are treated like friends by the Japanese soldiers, but afterward they become the worst enemies:

> During the entire time of the Japanese invasion, I remained with the red Karens in the mountains near Loikaw. Thus, I was always near the front, just three miles from the only usable road, kept open by the Japanese for a hasty retreat and their extreme, desperate defense. In the last six months of the war, at least 225,000 soldiers passed along this road, fleeing toward Thailand. They traveled at night, in companies of 5,000, either on foot or by whatever means of transportation they could find: cars, trucks, motorcycles, bicycles, ox carts, elephants, horses, mules. They were flowing in from all parts of Burma, chased by the victorious British and American armies. You can just imagine how we were "squeezed," being only three miles from the road. I couldn't escape, because this is an area where the forest is sparse; besides, I was determined to stay with the people as long as possible, to give help and comfort. So my life was at risk every day. No one in my village was killed, while in nearby villages many people were massacred by the Japanese, for the sheer joy of killing. But we were robbed of everything. They didn't leave us even a chicken, nor a pig, and very few oxen and cows. All of the rice was taken away.
>
> Then I was captured during the last month of the war by a particularly cruel officer, who was in command of the last Japanese squadron, from all appearances made up of thieves and murderers freed from jail and left for the final slaughter. I was tied up in their camp for a night and a day, and then, by what miracle I still don't know, I was freed. Then I had to run away and hide in the jungle.

On that occasion I was robbed of everything again. My Christians brought me some plates, a spoon, a little rice and one of their blankets, so that I could survive until the end of the war.

With Burma free of the Japanese and independent from England, Fr. Alfredo is able to return to Donoku in early January of 1947.

With fresh enthusiasm, he begins to rebuild everything that was destroyed and reorganize activities which were abandoned. "My life began again very quickly. First I had to open new schools, since everyone wants to be educated." He teaches catechism and English, cares for the sick, and takes up his pastoral activities.

Very soon, however, new trials appear. Burma has achieved independence, but the central government faces great obstacles: the Karen tribes, especially those composed of Baptists, are in rebellion, engaging in guerrilla warfare. The Catholics, loyal to the government and hated by the rebels, are afforded no protection by the regular army, which does not dare to send troops into areas controlled by the guerrillas.

Fr. Cremonesi, after a rebel attack in the village of Donoku, is forced to abandon his work and find refuge in Toungoo: "If only I could go back there! The worst that can happen is that I will be killed by the rebels. But the agony of these months is worse than any kind of death."

For Easter of 1952, a truce brings a bit of calm to the area, and he dares to return to Donoku. But the peace is short lived.

Even though they have been defeated, the rebels continue to make raids, even against villages where government troops are garrisoned. The regular army turns its rage on the Karen villages, all of which are suspected of harboring the rebels. Fr. Alfredo, while assisting his Christians, shares their dangers. He has obtained a pass from both sides to move about freely, but now he is suspected by the government troops, since he is determined to remain working in a guerrilla zone.

Thus, after the failure of a military operation by which the regular army had hoped to wrest complete control of the region from the rebels, the government troops, in retreat, suddenly burst into the village of Donoku, accusing Fr. Cremonesi and the villagers of aiding the rebels.

The conciliatory words of the father, seeking to reassure the soldiers and to defend the innocence of his people, are in vain. Filled with fury, the soldiers do not even allow him to finish speaking, but immediately begin firing their machine guns. They strike the village chieftain first, who is standing next to the missionary, and then turn their guns on Fr. Cremonesi. Struck full in the chest, he falls to the ground. It is February 7, 1953.

FR. PIETRO MANGHISI
(JANUARY 7, 1899 – FEBRUARY 15, 1953)

In Monopoli, 42 kilometers south of Bari, on January 7, 1899, the sixth of Luigi and Paolo Manghisi's twelve children is born into a family of farmers and agronomists.

Pietro is a lively youth, who loves to run and play with his friends in the barnyard or through the fields, where his father grows grapes, olives, and citrus trees. As soon as he finishes elementary school, he enters the seminary, but after only a couple of years, he must abandon his studies.

After the defeat of the Italian army in Caporetto by the Austrians on November 8, 1917, all the young men of his age, including 18-year-old Pietro, are sent to the front. Thus, unexpectedly, he spends Christmas of 1917 on Mount Asolone del Grappa, shivering in the cold, far from his loved ones, and deeply sad at heart. When his time at the front is completed, he is assigned to the office of "Damage Assessment" in Milan. By now, the seminary and his desire to study seem far away.

In Milan, even though he is still in the army, he does not live in the barracks, but rather has an apartment with some friends. After the long days bogged down by paperwork, he spends the evening playing cards or pool, going to the movies, the theater, or some other kind of show.

His life goes on with few cares, but Pietro is not happy. Unsatisfied and discouraged, he writes in his diary in July of 1920:

> So many thoughts are floating around in my head. I

am so annoyed and restless. Who will bring some light to my addled mind? I don't know what it is that's bothering me inside. What kind of life is in store for me? Who can let me know? There are so many things in life! So many illusions! So many lies!

He tries to take up some studies again on his own, in the hopes of attaining a secondary-school diploma, but the results of his exams are "a complete fiasco." He's twenty years old and he is anxious, tired, and exasperated because he can't seem to find his way.

The lack of the diploma, which would have opened up so many opportunities for him, puts him back to square one. Should he return to the seminary? Enroll in some courses? Go into business for himself? These are all questions he doesn't know how to answer.

In the fall of 1921, after having passed a make-up exam, he agrees with his father to enter the engineering school at the University of Bari. But on the very day he is to leave, he changes his mind again, this time for good. He has finally come to a firm decision and his restlessness seems to disappear: he will become a priest. Thus, he enters the Regional Pontifical Seminary of Molfetta.

His vocation, however, is not fully defined. On September 12 of 1922, he transfers to the Southern Seminary for Foreign Missions, in Ducenta. He had heard talk of this new seminary opened by Fr. Paolo Manna, and had even made a contribution to it, never planning actually to enroll. Many years later, he would write of those days:

> When Father Manna opened the seminary in Ducenta, I was a student in Molfetta. I don't know how, but I happened to come across his bulletin, *Propaganda Missionaria* (Missionary Promotion), in which there was a short appeal for contributions in order to furnish the seminary. I sent him a small donation. After a few days, I received a missionary postcard, on which was written: "Thank you for your offering. If you would also offer yourself, it would be even more appreciated." For me those words, rather crude in appearance, were like a lit-

tle flame which ignites a fire. In less than a year, I enrolled in Ducenta.

On June 6, 1925, having completed his theology studies in Milan, he is ordained a priest in the cathedral of Monopoli, and on the night of October 16, he sails from Naples for Kengtung, Burma, together with 14 other missionaries, among whom are Fr. Alfredo Cremonesi (assigned to Toungoo, Burma) and Fr. Antonio Barosi (assigned to Nanyang, China).

After a year and a half of language study in Kengtung, Fr. Pietro is assigned to Mong Ping, which would be his point of departure for visiting the villages spread throughout the jungle and mountains.

Life is difficult here; in June of 1927, he writes to his pastor:

> It's been a few days now that I've been in these impassable mountains, without any trails. The weather has been rainy and gray, which brings about boredom and crushes the spirit, already burdened by loneliness. If not for the love of God and the conversion of these poor souls, I wouldn't be able to live this life, even for a mountain of gold. You go up and down the mountains; you slip here, fall down there; you cross this stream and then the next. You pass through mud, open new trails, get drenched by a downpour, endure the searing rays of the sun, eat the best you can, rest whenever you are able, and move forward, always forward!
>
> Oh, your enthusiasm ends quickly, and how I wish that were the only problem!
>
> Adding to the heartbreak are the wounds you receive when you enter a village (and here, villages are made up of no more than 40 or 50 people) and watch the people run off like chickens before a hawk; and if they do welcome you into their homes, they surely don't want to hear anything about God. Today, for example, I was welcomed like a great man, because they knew I had medicine with me. Well, after I extracted a

tooth from an old man and put some medicine on a woman's arm, after talking about this and that, when the catechist (I can still not express myself well enough in the Mushò language) began to speak about God, the old folks began to fade away little by little, until I was left only with children, who had received some candy from me and were hoping for more. What a bitter disappointment! You go out with hope in your heart, and you return with your soul filled with sadness. Oh my God, have mercy on these poor souls, because if you do not stretch forth your hand, we are good for nothing.

But Fr. Manghisi doesn't give up. His deep faith and humility, nurtured in great fidelity to prayer, sustain him in his apostolate and help him to face any difficulty. Thus, his residence, in which he cares for those afflicted with typhoid and malaria, is always a happy place. His house overflows with orphans and abandoned children. He takes care of them, instructs, and teaches them. "If they are healthy and happy, the missionary shares their joy. But if I see them shivering from the cold, or sweating out the fever of malaria, I feel that pain too." With infinite patience and kindness, little by little Fr. Pietro begins to win the confidence and esteem of the entire Lahu population of the area.

He knows, though, that within the mission territory of Keng-tung, there are still many areas to reach, inhabited by tribes who have never seen a missionary. Up in the mountains are the Wa, a head hunting tribe. From the time when some British officials were beheaded by the Wa, their area has been declared off limits, even to missionaries. But Fr. Pietro considers them like "next door neighbors" and hopes one day to be able to know them, help them, evangelize them.

Finally in 1937, after much insistence, the British authorities give permission to open a new mission district among the Wa.

My heart leapt with joy, even if I had a little fear in meeting these Wa, who go on raiding parties in search of human heads, which they put on poles close to their villages, in offering to the spirits, so that they will protect their new crops of rice. But everything went well; my guardian angel was with me the whole time.

And so he settles in Mangphan, the capital of the Wa district, a large Buddhist village more than three thousand feet high. He builds a small hut of straw next to the salt sellers, and he waits.

He tries to speak with those he meets, begins to distribute medicine, care for the sick, and gather the abandoned children. In time, even the infamous headhunters come to love him. They help him to build a house, a dispensary, an orphanage, and later even a bamboo chapel!

He is well received and esteemed, but on June 21, 1940, he is forced to leave his new friends. Italy has declared war on England, and the Italian missionaries who live in the British colony of Burma, are suddenly considered enemies.

Even Fr. Manghisi, though isolated in the jungle, is accused by the British of fascist fanaticism. Considering him dangerous for his alleged anti-English propaganda, they force him to leave the mountains: "Oh you poor world, how ridiculous you are!" he writes in his journal. "What a fuss for a harmless missionary!" Yet, there is little to smile about. After being arrested, searched, and relieved of all his possessions, he is forbidden to return among the Wa.

But the worst is still to come. The war pervades everything, and the British government in Burma, foreseeing the Japanese invasion, decides to intern all Italian civilians in concentration camps in India. Any Italian missionary in Burma for less than ten years must leave his mission. Fr. Pietro Manghisi, who is a "veteran," is allowed to remain in Lashio, but he is condemned to complete inactivity.

After the British retreat, his position is no better with the new rulers, the Japanese, who suspect him of being a spy. Those in charge are the Kempetai, the infamous Japanese secret police, who torture and kill without compunction.

The very name Kempetai sends a chill up the spine.
For three long years everyone in Burma lived under this

terrible specter. Their long arms reached everywhere: no one was free from their terrible grip, not even the Japanese army nor their own generals; but we missionaries, because we are white and Christian, were particular targets of their wrath.

Fr. Manghisi himself gets to know the severity of this criminal gang and suffers their torture and insults. For five days he is harassed, slapped, and mistreated in every way, until he is finally released, but only after being forced to sign a confession to the Japanese army for causing trouble and promising not to tell anyone what has just happened to him.

Three years later, on April 15, 1945, the Japanese are defeated, and Fr. Pietro can return to Lashio. The city is completely destroyed and occupied by two American regiments and 25,000 Chinese soldiers. The American Catholics, after having built a wooden chapel, approach Fr. Manghisi to become their chaplain.

In December of 1948, Fr. Pietro is recalled to Italy in order to become rector of the seminary in Ducenta. The assignment does not please him, because he does not feel capable of doing the job well. He is not the type to be in charge, and he feels unprepared culturally. The long years of absence from Italy make him feel like a stranger in his own land. His reasoning is sound, but the superior, Fr. Manna, insists. In the end, out of obedience more than real conviction, he accepts. On April 24, 1949, after 24 years in the mission, he is in Ducenta, ready to begin a new life.

His stay at the seminary is really very short, although long enough to leave rich and affectionate memories among the students. After Burma's declaration of independence on January 4, 1948, the political situation has worsened. The government, reasoning that the rebellion of the northern tribes is being helped by enemy agents, issues extremely restrictive rules in regard to foreigners entering the country.

The Italian missionaries are no exceptions to these rules. Beginning in 1949, only those who have obtained their visa prior to 1930 can re-enter the country. In Italy, the only one who qualifies is Fr.

Manghisi. Thus, in January of 1950, he returns to Burma and is assigned to Namtu, once again in the Karen mountains.

> There is much misery here. During the rebel fighting, I have had deaths among my Christians, including a catechist. Now we are afraid of being overrun by the Chinese communists. Already many Chinese have fled here from the famine and taxes in China. In our Kengtung mission area, Chinese nationalist troops have spread out through the mountains, bringing hunger and fear.

Lashio, the district to which Fr. Pietro is transferred in 1951, is close to the Chinese border, and even more subject to the raids of the Chinese irregulars. Lacking provisions and pay, they turn to banditry, looting, and destroying Karen villages. The Karens, in order to defend themselves, establish a contingent of troops, with the support of the government.

Fr. Manghisi, in spite of the difficult situation, dedicates himself to caring for the wounded. He knows the dangers he is facing, but he cannot help but remain close to his people. Thus, often he finds himself right in the field of battle.

On February 15, 1953, while approaching the border by jeep, he is ambushed by Chinese guerrillas. The jeep driver recounts the incident:

> In the morning, Father celebrated Mass for the soldiers in the Nampaka camp, and then immediately continued his journey toward the border. Father wanted to drive the jeep, and I sat next to him. Along the road we picked up two old women and a baby.
>
> At mile marker 91, north of Lashio, while the jeep was crossing a bridge, a volley of machine gun fire began from a nearby hill. I jumped out of the jeep and rolled under the bridge to safety, but the machine gun fire continued furiously.
>
> The jeep slowed down, and just after reaching the

far side of the bridge, Father fell on the berm of the road with two bullets in his head, while the jeep continued on and crashed into the mountain. A dozen Chinese guerrillas hurried down the hill and onto the jeep. Coming out of hiding, I ran to Father, who recognized me, moved his lips, opened his eyes wide, and died.

Then I begged the guerrillas to help me carry the body away, but they threatened me with the machine guns and said, "Leave the dead where they are and take off, if you value your skin…"

In 1962, at mile marker 91 of the Burma Road, a white cross and headstone were erected, reminding passersby of the martyrdom of Fr. Pietro Manghisi and testifying to his fidelity to the missionary vocation.

FR. ELIODORO FARRONATO
(MAY 18, 1912 – DECEMBER 11, 1955)

It is October 10, 1926. The Church of St. Mary Major in Treviso is jammed with people. Fr. Antonio Farronato has just finished celebrating the Mass and is saying goodbye to his family and friends, as he prepares to leave for Burma with his confreres. As he comes down from the pulpit the first person he greets is one of his eight brothers, Eliodoro, who attends the minor seminary in the diocese of Thiene.

There has always been a strong bond between the two. Eliodoro has followed the progress of his brother, whom he loves and respects as a model, and has paid close attention to every stage of Antonio's journey, because ever since he was very young, he somehow knew that they would share the same vocation. Now that Antonio is leaving for Burma, Eliodoro "follows" him in his mind, confident that one day he will be able to embrace him once again.

Eliodoro is an energetic youth, and very decisive. Even though he is only 14 years old, he already has clear ideas about his life. Thus, after two years, he enters the P.I.M.E. seminary in Monza. On his desk in study hall there is always displayed a letter from Mong Yong. It's from Antonio, who writes to him in August of 1929:

> Dear brother, here I live without a house, I get up without an alarm clock, I pray without a church, I hunt without a license, I am happy without friends, I study languages without teachers, I have no days without struggles, I grow old without anyone noticing it, I will die without regrets... When are you going to come and join me?

Even though his parents are against the idea of having another son so far away and in constant danger, Eliodoro can't wait to finish his seminary studies and go to be with his brother. But on October 13, 1931, that dream seems to die. Antonio, his big brother and best friend, succumbs to malaria in his Burmese village, at the age of 30. Eliodoro cries like a baby, but he has the strength to confide to his companions: "I was hoping that I would go to help him, but if it is God's will, I will go to replace him."

And so, on September 22, 1934, Eliodoro is ordained a priest, and is assigned to Burma, to the very mission where his brother was working.

On the evening of August 24, 1935, he sails for the Orient, and the next day, from the deck of the ship, he writes to his family:

> At the moment of departure the sea and the sky seemed dreary, almost as if to match the sadness of the one who was leaving and the ones who were staying. But above the light clouds there was the sun, beautiful as always, and today it is shining brightly. If I have left you behind, it is for God. Thus, after the sadness, I feel an inexpressible joy. And I hope that you can feel it too; there is no happier person than I! It has been worth all the sacrifices I have made in leaving everything behind, to know the consolation of belonging only to God, to love Him, and bring others to love Him!

Having arrived in Burma, after a period of studying the Shan language, he goes to Mong Yong in April of 1936; the people are already expecting him, and he dives into his pastoral activity.

But soon, because he is tall and strong, with the muscular body common to the farmers of his homeland, he is assigned to the district of Mong-tsat, the most distant and difficult, in eastern Burma, about one week on horseback from Kengtung. The road is practically impassable, winding through the forests and climbing up the mountains. In some places it becomes nothing more than a trail, often overgrown with vegetation, so that he has to hack out a new way by axe.

After arriving in the isolated village, he becomes bricklayer, cook, farmer, and tailor. He builds churches, orphanages, clinics, and schools.

His confreres admire Fr. Eliodoro, not only because he works hard in such a difficult environment, but above all because he is so loved and respected by all of the Shan and Lahu inhabitants, due to his great characteristics of humanity and love.

In 1940, the missionaries of Kengtung begin to feel the repercussions of the war, and finally they are confined by the British in isolation zones. The first place of confinement is the mission residence of Kengtung, where Fr. Eliodoro organizes professional schools for the missionaries forced into inactivity. Thus, besides filling the empty time, they learn new skills, such as mechanics and photography. Fr. Farronato takes advantage of the opportunity to augment his medical knowledge.

After a year, Fr. Eliodoro and the other missionaries are transferred to Kalò, and in 1942, they are moved to internment camps in India, at Katapahar, in the foothills of the Himalayas. From here, they are taken to Deoli in Rajasthan. Finally, in 1943, they are all gathered in the general camp of Dhera Dun, with hundreds of other missionaries. Fr. Eliodoro is number 18522.

He is freed in 1944, and his greatest desire is to return to Kengtung as soon as possible, but he does not receive the permission of the British, since Burma is still under the control of the Japanese. He remains in Bezwada, India, where he organizes a dispensary for the outcastes.

When the war is over in 1946, he can return to Kengtung and he suffers a hard blow: the mission of Mong-tsat has been completely destroyed, and he has to start over from scratch. But as he begins to rebuild, even though it is very tiring, he is always full of dreams, courage, and intuition. In fact, at that very time the church in Burma is beginning to realize that evangelization efforts will be much stronger if the various languages, only spoken up to now, are given an alphabet. Fr. Eliodoro is assigned the task to study the languages of the Burmese tribes, and he ends up becoming "the best linguist in the mission." Thus, he begins to translate prayers, scripture, catechism, and liturgical songs into the Shan, Lahu and Akhà languages.

But his work is not finished here. In fact (and this may be the greatest manifestation of his initiative and intelligence), the mountain tribes are not the only targets of evangelization; also the higher social classes must be reached. To this end, Fr. Eliodoro begins to compile a catechism in Khun, that ancient language spoken by the dynastic kings and used in the sacred texts preserved for centuries in the shrines of the country. A Catholic catechism in this language requires years of dedication to transcribe and compile: a "sweet struggle" as Fr. Eliodoro describes it.

In September of 1955 he returns to Kengtung and while at the Bishop's residence he finishes the final draft of the catechism, preparing it for definitive approval. At the end of November, this important work is completed: "Now I will take a long break," he writes to his cousin.

> I'm getting ready to return to my residence, which unfortunately is still occupied by the troops of the Burmese government; they've kindly consented to allow me the use of the second floor of the house. It would certainly be better if the soldiers were not there! Anyway, I'll try to do a little bit of good for them too, in return for the evil they are doing.

Thus, at the beginning of December, 1955, Fr. Eliodoro is ready to go to Mong Yong, where he plans to celebrate Christmas with his Christian community. The Burmese soldiers lodged in his house promise him safe passage in one of their military trucks, but then they leave without him. So, on December 4, making use of public transportation, Fr. Farronato heads out for Mong Pyak, where Fr. Cattani is living, about halfway to Mong Yong.

Three days later, although warned by everyone about the danger that could await him on the road, he continues his journey on horseback, accompanied by three men.

On the morning of December 9, he can already see Mong Yong in the distance. He has crossed through forests and mountains infested with brigands and now, his heart in his throat, he looks down at his village from above. He thinks he can see his house, and thirty meters farther along, separated by small ravine, the grave of his brother. So much time has passed, yet every person and event come back vividly to his mind. He takes a deep breath. Another ten kilometers and he will be home.

But as soon as he starts on his way again, he is stopped by 17 Chinese guerrillas. Before he can even react, he is tied up and taken back a half mile into the jungle. It is December 11, 1955.

For some days the Burmese soldiers and the people of the village search for him. On the evening of the fourteenth, they find his body buried under some rocks in a stream bed. The body has three bullet wounds in the chest and one in the neck; the arms and neck are covered with rope burns. No one knows why he was killed, nor by whom. Maybe it was the nationalist Chinese soldiers who, after the murder, continued their wandering through the mountains.

Eliodoro is buried next to his brother, and both of their graves are witnesses of faith among the isolated villages of Burma.

BANGLADESH: THE UNKNOWN COUNTRY

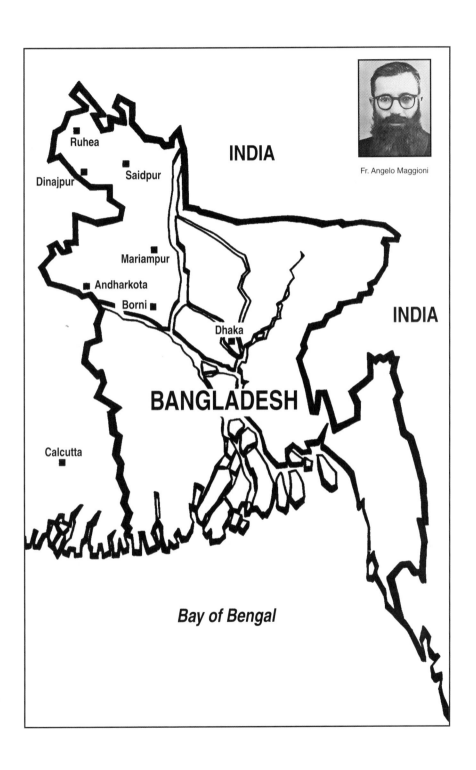

Ruhea

Saidpur

Dinajpur

INDIA

Mariampur

Andharkota

Borni

Dhaka

INDIA

BANGLADESH

Calcutta

Bay of Bengal

Fr. Angelo Maggioni

INTRODUCTION

By Fr. Angelo Rusconi

BANGLADESH: I WATCHED IT BEING BORN ONE WINTER AFTERNOON. IT was 4:30 p.m. on December 16, 1971, when the army of Pakistan signed an unconditional surrender. The Hindus and Moslems of the district of Jonail reserved for me, a missionary, the honor and emotion of raising the flag of the new nation for the first time.

It was a touching gesture of gratitude for the fact that the mission had always been there for them. As in all other parts of the country, the Catholic church, though small in number, had become a "Noah's ark," a welcoming place of refuge, open to all.

That new flag was, and is, extremely simple, with just two colors: a large red circle (symbol of the blood that has been poured out lavishly, generously, by the people, the intellectuals, the youth) on a field of green, reminiscent of the appearance of the country during the monsoon season.

At the end of British rule in 1947, East Pakistan was never really considered a part of a unified nation by West Pakistan. Rather, it was more like a distant province, or a colony, to be exploited for its rice, jute, and sugar cane. It reached the point that "Urdu and only Urdu" (the language of West Pakistan) was declared the national language.

It was truly consoling to see millions of people, without face or name, for centuries divided and split into so many religious and social factions, taking up the awareness and will to be one people, dreaming of great things, and singing their anthem: "Golden Bengal, I love you; your blue sky, your wind, the aroma of your mango trees, your smiling fields, fill me with joy." Because they were without weapons, armed only with sticks, they were crushed. "Weeping and mourning, the country cannot be consoled, because her sons are no longer here." Not a single human right was respected. Blind and furious repression spread from south to north. It is said that three million people were killed. The support of India was significant, heavy, intentional. There was the terrible feeling of being all alone, unimportant to the great powers. Martial law became more rigorous as the interim government became more ineffective. Their leader was in prison in West Pakistan. Civil disobedience became almost unbearable; private vendettas caused fear everywhere. And then ten million refugees began an exodus of biblical proportions toward India.

I remember having written, quoting Tagore: "How many times, mother, I have opened the door and looked out into the darkness. I can't see anything. I'm beginning to doubt whether there's still a road out there at all."

The growth of the new nation was also torturous: a series of coups, recurring cyclones and floods, hunger and disease, almost always ignored by the rest of the world. "Who has ever heard of Bangladesh?" was the title of an editorial in the French newspaper, *Le Monde*. One hundred and ten million people count for nothing!

The fragility of the coastal zone, constantly exposed to cyclones and floods, is an apt symbol for the precarious socio-political situation of the country as well.

In 1975, Sheikh Mujib Rahman, the father of the country, the "bongobondhu," the friend of Bengal, was murdered, together with his whole family. There was an attempt to restore some order to the chaos through the imposition of martial law, but the military was divided. After a failed coup, the popular referendum of 1977 brought the young general Ziaur Rahaman to power. His party then gained two thirds of the parliamentary seats in the election of 1978.

Zia (as he was commonly known) had three steps to his plan to move the country toward democracy: a "green revolution" consisting in large scale construction of canals for irrigation and water control; an industrial revolution and the mechanization of agriculture; and an educational revolution, working toward literacy. While following an international policy of nonalignment, Ziaur moved the society toward a return to the spirit of Islam, as is expressed in the four principles of the national philosophy: "faith in and absolute fidelity to Allah, nationalism, democracy, socialism."

On May 30, 1981, Ziaur was assassinated by a small group of his own officers. Elections the following November did nothing to fill the vacuum of power, and "for reasons of security," the military took command of the country. The cabinet and parliament were dissolved, the constitution suspended, and martial law was once again strictly imposed. General Ershad, the strongman of the moment, installed a presidential regime which became more and more repressive, until in 1987, all civil laws were suspended and a curfew was imposed upon the major cities.

The opposition, a collection of 21 parties, demanded Ershad's resignation. The leaders of the protest were two women, jailed along with thousands of demonstrators. Begum Khaleda Zia (45 years old), president of the National Party of Bangladesh, is the widow of Ziaur Rahaman, assassinated in 1981. Sheika Hazina Wajed (43 years old), president of the Awami League, is the daughter of the first president. Someone wrote that these two women were "a balanced mix of Western action and Islamic attitude, of political ambition and martyrdom; tragic heroines, who work to see that the blood of their family members was not shed in vain." In February of 1991, in the context of a general strike and violent riots, Ershad was forced to resign and was immediately arrested on charges of illegal possession of arms, corruption, and embezzlement.

The next political phase began with a surprise. In the country's first democratic elections (February 27, 1991), Khaleda Zia was elected and her National Party of Bangladesh won an absolute majority in Parliament with 140 seats.

The Awami League, so popular right after independence, was left with 90 seats; the surprisingly modest 35 seats won by the Islamic Party indicate that fundamentalism, stimulated on the Indian subcontinent by the Gulf War, has not made inroads beyond a few sporadic episodes.

If the tenacity of the opposition to General Ershad has been rewarded, the problems of Bangladesh remain, and require much more than talk to be resolved.

Such is the country in the dramatic and glorious years of independence. To this country Fr. Angelo Maggioni devoted himself at the cost of his own life. Four other priests would also die. Tagore sings: "I have made a gift of my life; glory to God."

FR. ANGELO MAGGIONI
(JUNE 14, 1917 – AUGUST 14, 1972)

December 16, 1971. Finally, after nine months of civil war, the trapped and defeated Pakistanis sign a truce with the Bengalis. With the resulting secession from West Pakistan, Bangladesh is born. Exhausted by the destruction of the war, overpopulation, and famine, the country must start over again from nothing.

> In these months, so many things have been happening! So many beautiful and ugly events, but the bad outweighs the good: the flight of our Christian and non-Christian villagers to escape the reprisals of the Pakistani soldiers, destruction of entire villages, looting, indiscriminate killing of innocent people, and then the war of liberation. Here around the mission of Andharkota, along the Ganges River, for twenty miles all the villages have been burned by the soldiers on the pretext that they were hiding Bengali guerrillas. Not only that: in every village, they took a certain number of old people and children who were not able to escape, made them dig a pit, and then shot them...
>
> Most of the people, filled with fear and uncertainty about what was happening, ran here and there looking for safety... No one would take them in; the fear was too great. They sold everything, all their cows and rice, then left their homes and ran away. Many crossed the border.

Now that victory has been won and nine months of sacrifices have been rewarded, they are coming back. And so the real problems begin. These people are returning with nothing and to nothing: no house (those not burned or looted have been destroyed by the weather and flooding), no work tools, no means of livelihood (they have neither cows nor oxen to plow the fields). Last year they were not able to harvest and store anything… How will all of these people manage to live?

It's a disturbing question which gives Fr. Angelo Maggioni no peace. From farmers' stock, he knows only too well what it means to have no harvest. His thoughts go back a few years. How many times did his family have to "tighten their belts" because the produce of the rented fields in Trezzo, along the Adda river, had been meager or had gone bad?

He knows well his father's struggle to provide for his family, so much so that his sister, while still a child, had to work in the textile mills of the area, with intolerable hours and conditions. He remembers how any extra expense was simply impossible. He was able to enter the P.I.M.E. seminary at the age of 11 only because the rector waived the tuition fee. He also remembers the despair of his mother when she could not buy medicine to treat the sickness which would kill his father back in 1929. And how can he forget the five straight years in which he did not see his family, because he couldn't afford a trip home from the seminary in Treviso and they had no means to come and visit him?

With this same spirit of sacrifice, developed in such great poverty, now, after 32 years of priesthood and 23 years in Bengal, he can face suffering and injustice, sharing in the poverty and hardships of his adopted people. His goodness and humility impress all who meet him.

His sister Rosa recalls:

If he ever lost his patience, no one even realized it. He was good, truly good. He has never been an irritable type of person. He always wore a smile, even when he was burdened by many worries. And he was never able to be tough with anyone.

In the mission, facing so many abuses and trials, he suffers silently, showing in a thousand ways his care and Christian solidarity with everyone. This is the way that he touched people: with his meekness, his calm smile, his quiet speech, and humble attitude. A Bengali teacher in the high school of Andharkota, learning of his death, said as she dried her tears: "This priest of yours embodies the idea that we Muslims have of sanctity. We are strong in faith, but rarely do we also achieve humility; he was able to blend these two qualities."

Fr. Angelo Maggioni, born in 1917 in Trezzo d'Adda, in the province of Milan, was ordained a P.I.M.E. priest at the age of 22. World War II prevented him from going to the missions immediately. The borders of Italy were closed, and only those on military maneuvers were permitted to go abroad. Thus, for nine years, Fr. Angelo worked in the parish of Fara D'Adda, waiting for his departure to Bangladesh (then called East Pakistan), to which he had already been assigned.

In 1948, he is finally able to leave. Together with four other confreres assigned to the same mission, he sails on the *Taurina*, a decommissioned warship now used as a freighter. After 33 days of travel, they finally touch Bengali soil on November 14. The veteran missionaries are there to welcome them: "Gaunt and yellow with malaria, they looked at us and their eyes were full of joy. To them, we were the assurance that the mission would continue; we had all been waiting ten years for this moment." New forces, and new hope have arrived.

It has only been one year since Great Britain granted independence to the Indian subcontinent, which was divided into two states, along religious lines: India, with a predominantly Hindu population, and Pakistan, split into two sections, 1500 kilometers apart and inhabited primarily by Muslims.

It is a partition made by outsiders, and the real losers have always been the Bengalis. East Pakistan, in fact, lost its capital, the great city of Calcutta, and now finds itself not only surrounded by the huge country of India, but also in a situation of exploitation and absolute dependence upon the flourishing industries of West Pakistan. Thus, Fr. Maggioni begins and develops his pastoral work in the poorest and most populated area of this fractured empire, among Bengali Muslims, 80 percent of whom are illiterate farmers.

His first assignment is the mission of Ruhea, assisting an Indian pastor. Then he goes to Mariampur where he learns the Santal language in order to be able to communicate with the tribes of the nearby villages. In fact, this work among the tribals becomes his principal activity. Even in the other places to which he is transferred (Borni, Saidpur, Dinajpur, and finally Andharkota), he does not build great structures, nor dedicate himself to the construction of health and education facilities; rather, he devotes himself to quiet work among the tribal Santals, forming small Christian communities and offering his spiritual and material help.

He is convinced that the "weariness" of these people is due to malnutrition.

> They never eat enough; rice is the staple, often the only food, and sometimes they don't even have that. The humid heat, which often goes over 100 degrees, brings about such exhaustion that all you want to do is drink and sleep. As soon as it becomes a bit more bearable, the rainy season begins, and then it is simply endless water. Not only the fields, but also the roads are flooded, huts are damaged and the rice crop goes bad. Then the dry months return, with inexorable heat and inevitable famine.

This vicious cycle of dry heat and flooding make it difficult to maintain consistent and fruitful farmlands. Fr. Maggioni, therefore, organizes systems of irrigation, to guarantee water in the dry months and to reduce flooding in the rainy season.

Since 1948, Fr. Angelo has returned to Italy only twice: in 1961 and 1971. During this last vacation at the home of his sister Rosa he learns from the Italian newspapers of the tragic news about East Pakistan. President Yahya Khan has ordered bloody reprisals against the separatists of Bengal, who have proclaimed the Republic of Bangladesh on March 26, 1971. The civil war forces 10 million people to become refugees and arouses the intervention of India in defense of the Bengalis. Fr. Maggioni receives troubling news from Andharkota, and immediately fixes the date for his return. His sister tries to dissuade him, but there is nothing she can do to change his mind. Rosa recalls:

> I said to him: "Why go? Stay here at least until the situation has calmed down some. You're not going to be able to change anything anyway."
> "I know," he replied in his usual calm way, "but I have to go. I'm the oldest one in the mission. I know how to resolve certain problems."

Thus, without thinking twice, Fr. Maggioni returns to Bangladesh, to his mission of Andharkota. He finds several villages burned and looted and feels compelled to go to great lengths to save Christians and Hindus. For his protection of the poor and defenseless, he is himself harassed and mistreated. But he prefers not to write home about all the things that are happening. He gives only some general indications about the shape of the country, as in his letter of October 26, 1971:

> The situation is always precarious, and always worsening, like a bubble which can burst at any moment. It is this atmosphere of uncertainty which keeps us constantly in suspense. We cannot make any plans for the future, because we have no idea what the future will be. Faith in God: this is what sustains us.

Then, for several months, his family in Italy receives no news. It's only in January of 1972 that another letter arrives, in which he speaks of the enormous destruction and three million dead since the start of the civil war. With the arrival of the Indians, a new spiral of violence begins against West Pakistanis in Bengali territory, against those who look Pakistani, or against anyone whom it was convenient to consider Pakistani. There are lynchings and throat slashings along the road.

Three missionaries are also murdered, among whom is the Bengali priest, Fr. Lucas, killed by a rifle shot to the neck.

Then in the spring, rebuilding slowly begins. Everything is razed to the ground. Houses, streets, schools, canals, bridges have all been destroyed.

The prime minister of the new Bengali state, Mujbur Rahman, accepts humanitarian and economic aid from wherever he can get it. International Catholic relief agencies, in agreement with the government of Dhaka, institute incentives for self-reliance among the Bengalis and help to provide at least the basic necessities of life.

Fr. Maggioni is pastor in Andharkota, but he dedicates himself mostly to pastoral work in the forty villages spread throughout the territory of his parish. Here he comes into contact with the refugees returning from India, who "live in tents, in makeshift huts of straw and leaves, or simply under the trees. My heart breaks to see the conditions of so many people without a home, without work, without food." He can't say no to anyone.

> All day long my house is filled with the commotion of people asking for help: one wants help to build his house, another wants clothes, or a bit of rice or corn; some women ask for powdered milk for their babies; some want money to help them buy an ox; others want us to put a water pump or well their village, because they don't have potable water.

The mission becomes a center of collection and distribution. It is the only social organization that is functioning.

> Armed bands roam the countryside, committing all kinds of robberies. The residences of the missionaries, often set off by themselves, are the most vulnerable to the attacks of the brigands, because they are the places where goods from outside agencies are stored and distributed.

This is precisely what happens in the case of Fr. Angelo.

It is 1:00 a.m. on August 14, 1972. A band of robbers, armed with rifles, breaks into the mission of Andharkota. On the first floor porch, three Christian youths are sleeping peacefully. The thieves shout and scream for Fr. Angelo. Waking with a start, he goes out. Before he can even light the lantern, two shots are fired at him. He flees back into the house. Meanwhile, two of the boys on the porch escape, but the third is captured and commanded to tell where the money is. He doesn't know. The thieves rush to the upper floor and turn the house upside down. More shots are heard. The people of the nearby village cry out in fear, but no one has the courage to intervene. After 45 minutes the robbers run off, disappointed in not having found the few hundred rupees which Fr. Angelo had brought from the bank the day before. The sisters and neighbors hurry to the house, but Fr. Angelo is already dead, lying in the middle of his room. A bullet shot through a crack in the door has struck his aorta.

THE PHILIPPINES:
A DIALOGUE OF
MANY VOICES

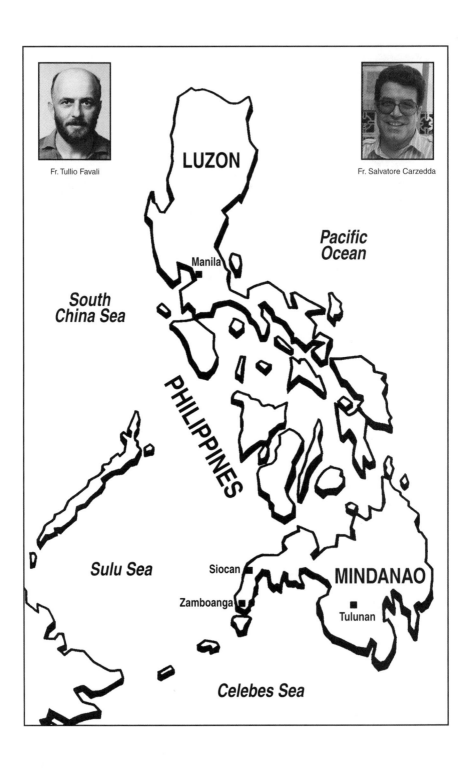

Fr. Tullio Favali

Fr. Salvatore Carzedda

LUZON

Pacific
Ocean

Manila

South
China Sea

PHILIPPINES

Sulu Sea

Siocan

MINDANAO

Zamboanga

Tulunan

Celebes Sea

INTRODUCTION

By Fr. Giorgio Licini

THE ISLAND OF MINDANAO, THE LARGEST IN THE SOUTHERN PHILIP-pines and second largest in the entire archipelago, suffered the most from the social and political tensions gripping the country in the second half of the twentieth century. While the anti-colonial struggle against Spain in the late 1800s was concentrated around Manila on the northern island of Luzon, the more recent battles among opposing forces of the Philippine society were fought mostly in the central and southern areas. In Luzon, America exercised significant control with its largest military bases in Asia, Clark naval base and Subic Bay air base, a control which indirectly extends to the entire archipelago and throughout southeast Asia.

On September 23, 1972, President Ferdinand Marcos declared martial law, citing as justification the double threat of communist guerrillas and Muslim separatists.

It is difficult to deny the real dangers posed by these two forces. The Vietnam war was fought close to the Philippines, with America in difficulty and the Soviet Union making no attempt to hide its imperialistic ambitions (the U.S. left the bases in the Philippines only in 1991, after the Gorbachev "revolution" and the worldwide failure of Marxism). The Muslims, for their part, had to be taken seriously. During the late seventies, they openly sought secession of Mindanao and some surrounding islands. Martial law, however, did not bring the peace it promised.

The Philippine army became abusive and oppressive toward civilians. Meanwhile, Marcos developed a political and financial oligarchy which was concerned only with its own interests — an easy target for the communist propaganda of social justice, equal opportunity, national independence, and the redistribution of land to the farmers.

Ferdinand Marcos and his attractive wife Imelda Romualdez were living in wanton luxury, but at the same time, with that populist style typical of all dictators, pretended to help the poor. In this way they won the support of the most miserable sectors of society and reduced the influence of the opposition. Ferdinand was intelligent, perhaps more so than all the previous Philippine presidents. Imelda was dynamic and energetic, capable of winning admiration both locally and internationally.

The Marcoses and their cronies were terrified of the armed communists of the "New People's Army" which did not hesitate to use brutal threats and methods. With the Muslims, on the other hand, the government was able to reach an agreement for the autonomy of 13 southern provinces; but the treaty, signed in Tripoli in 1976, had no concrete follow-up.

The Christian portion of the population, supported by the army, was vigorously opposed not only to the secession of Mindanao but also to the idea of Muslim administration in territories which had a Christian majority.

The Catholic Church, to which more than 80 percent of the Filipinos belong, did not remain distant from these conflicts. Cardinal Jaime Sin of Manila initiated a relationship of "critical collaboration" with the government, making public statements of either approval or fierce criticism, which had significant effect upon those in power.

At the same time, Base Christian Communities began to develop, which brought about popular awareness of the abuses of the dictatorship. Many Christians began to support the organizations of the left. Some priests, especially in the countryside, took up arms and joined the rebels. The Association of Major Religious Superiors openly declared itself on the side of the oppressed.

The diocese of Kidapawan, on the island of Mindanao, formed only in 1976, distinguished itself nationally for the work of consciousness-raising and formation of the people toward a just and equal society. Under the guidance first of Bishop Ferdinando Escaler and then Bishop Orlando Quevedo, the Base Christian Communities began to challenge the interests of the local powers and the foreign multinationals. The Christian population was composed mostly of Ilongo immigrants from the central island of Panay, very determined people, quick to make friends, but also fiercely resistant when pushed by conflicts which affected them personally.

This is the context in which Fr. Tullio Favali was killed on April 11, 1985. In reality, it was a devastating incident also for the Marcos dictatorship. The protests of the international community were loud and long. In front of the American ambassador, Marcos ordered the deaths of the Manero brothers, who murdered Fr. Tullio. This order would not be carried out, but by now the patience of Cardinal Sin was worn thin. A month later, at the memorial service for Fr. Favali, he lashed out directly at the dictator: "Enough of these dirty tricks!" Marcos then moved up the presidential elections to February of 1986; he won through obvious fraud, but then was forced into exile in Hawaii, where he died three year later.

In 1986, Cory Aquino (widow of Benigno Aquino, who was assassinated upon return from exile in the U.S.) became the first woman president in the history of Philippines. Not only was the dictatorship over, but the insurrection of the left, which had boycotted her, began to decline. Aquino dedicated herself to rebuilding the civil and political structures of the country. She re-opened Parliament and promulgated a new constitution. She sought peace treaties with the communists rebels and Muslim separatists, but without success.

Fidel Ramos, who had served first as Secretary of State and then Defense Minister under Aquino, succeeded her as president in 1992, after relatively calm national elections, but not without significant doubts about irregularities during the interminable and controversial process of counting the votes. And while the country was waiting for the result of the polls on the evening of May 20, 1992, unknown killers shot Fr. Salvatore Carzedda, another P.I.M.E. missionary dedicated to interreligious dialogue in Zamboanga City (western Mindanao) within the *Silsilah* ("Chain") movement founded in 1984 by his confrere and friend, Fr. Sebastiano D'Ambra.

Indeed, Christian and Muslims in the southern part of the Philippines had been struggling against one another since at least the early seventies. The Muslims, numbering around three million, have occupied the territory since before the arrival of the Spanish 400 years ago. The Christians, on the other hand, immigrated to the area after World War II, seeking a "new frontier" from the poverty and overpopulation of other islands.

At first, the locals had freely ceded some land to the newcomers, for very little money and with no concern for legalities, property titles, etc. The land in question was uncultivated, forested area, which would have to be cut in order to provide fields for farming. Today, they accuse the Christians of having invaded their island, and they want all or most of the land back. In the seventies and eighties they dreamed of secession and the creation of an independent state; now they seem content to have significant autonomy, which the government seems willing to concede.

The motives for killing Fr. Salvatore remain obscure even today; but it seems certain that political and religious motivations were tangled together, as is always the case when we speak of the "Islamic question."

Others have shared the fate of Fr. Salvatore during the first months of Ramos' presidency in the second half of 1992: lay and religious, Catholic and Protestant, Filipinos and foreigners. There has also been the kidnapping of Catholic and Evangelical missionaries in Basilan and Sulu, the southernmost islands, by a group of extremists, trained in Arab countries, who call themselves *Abu Sayyaf*. They accuse the Christians of attempting to destroy Islam.

A real puzzle, this island of Mindanao. There is not just one conflict, but many different ones, in which it becomes obligatory to take sides. There are those who have chosen armed struggle, and they are dead. There are those who have chosen the path of dialogue and peace, and they are dead as well.

FR. TULLIO FAVALI

(DECEMBER 10, 1946 – APRIL 11, 1985)

> I am a young man from Mantua, nearly 32 years old, and I would like to enter P.I.M.E. to serve the church as a missionary priest. Let me begin by saying that I spent the years of my youth in the diocesan seminary, up to a year and a half before ordination. In 1970 I interrupted my journey in order to follow a different path... My superiors tried to dissuade me, but I wanted to make up my own mind; thus, I tried, with difficulty, to insert myself into the world.

This is just one excerpt from the long letter sent by Tullio Favali to the superior of P.I.M.E. in 1978, expressing his desire, by now more than well founded, to become a missionary priest.

Having entered the diocesan seminary of Mantua at the age of 11, Tullio leaves just before he is to be ordained, to spend eight years in different fields of work and study.

It is the seventies, the post-conciliar age, still reverberating from the worldwide unrest of 1968. Many young men in the seminary from their childhood feel the need to clarify the identity of the priest, and Tullio is one of these. He needs, as he puts it,

> a discernment in regard to celibacy; a search for independence and an autonomous life outside of a protected environment, one that requires concrete choices and action; something that goes beyond purely intellectual pursuits; solidarity with the poorest of the poor, shar-

ing their hard lot. Then there's also the fear of becoming a priest, conscious as I am of my own limitations. I feel somewhat powerless in the face of an overwhelming world. I don't have the heart of a lion, enabling me to impose myself on others.

Thus, he struggles with the Lord for many years. He hesitates to become a priest, not because he doesn't feel the call, but because of the difficulties he foresees. He fears the loneliness of a rectory in the midst of indifferent parishioners; he wants to share in the daily life of authentic and spontaneous people; he wants to try his hand at manual work; he feels the desire to have a family.

In 1970, then, he leaves the seminary. However, he makes no break with his faith; rather he chairs the liturgy commission of his parish, he teaches catechism to the children, he is involved in Catholic Action and participates in the youth group.

Soon, however, he has to leave for military service (mandatory for all young men in Italy), first in Palermo and then in Torino. He could have entered as a noncommissioned officer, thus earning more money to help his impoverished family. But he asks to be enlisted as a simple soldier, with no special privileges. This attitude would be a constant throughout his entire life.

After his discharge, he finds work in a textile factory, but this job doesn't last long. His boss is an unjust and arbitrary man. Tullio is not sure how to react and finally decides simply to seek work elsewhere. This is the first of many job changes. He works for a while in a dairy, and then as a welder, but these too leave him disillusioned, as he sees his coworkers being used as political pawns, thrown into a hard and often unjustified struggle. For one summer, he also works as a waiter on Lake Como.

Meanwhile, back at home, people are talking. They say that he has an unstable character, that he is untrustworthy. His widowed mother wishes that her son would finally settle down into a secure job, marry a fine woman and raise a family. Basically he is a young man like so many others, perhaps a bit more idealistic than most, more thirsting for God, undergoing a relentless, agonizing search for his way. Surely, he loves old people and children; he stops to talk with everyone, even the young men who hang out at the bars and don't go to church; he accepts everyone without prejudice. He would like, maybe, to be a gypsy, meeting people all over the world, picking them up along the way and forming a caravan of all the people he loves.

Meanwhile, the priestly vocation he has tried to forget comes ever stronger to the surface. It takes on a more defined shape, however, developed in the years of service to his parish and in long talks with his friends: the mission *ad gentes*, to those who do not know Christ.

Tullio decides to leave his job in the factory. For a while he remains unemployed, and then gains a job as a public employee in the community of Sustinente, his hometown. He has also earned a degree in geometry by attending night school.

His mother is happy now, but Tullio could never spend his life behind a desk in city hall. He has been playing games with the Lord for too long. "In all this time," he writes, "I was neglecting my spiritual life a bit, wanting to divest myself of all my clerical 'habits'. Thus, little by little I began to feel empty, to lose my identity. But I could never fully cast off that which was the very substance of my life." Now sure of his priestly and missionary vocation, he returns to the seminary of Mantua to speak with the rector.

At the same time, he is in contact with P.I.M.E., which he knows through its magazines, and he goes to Busto Arsizio, where the institute has a house of formation and vocational discernment. His decision amazes everyone. But Tullio is finally serene; he has his choice clearly before him, without any more doubts or hesitations. His friends notice the difference: "He was completely changed; what we saw before us was a man, a true man." What strikes everyone the most is his interior peace, the fruit of deep maturity.

On October 1, 1978, he enters the P.I.M.E. seminary in Monza, willingly starting his theological studies over from the beginning, because it has been so long since his previous seminary days. It is a beautiful sign of his humility and openness: at the age of 32 he returns to the desk, to repeat the courses he had almost finished eight years earlier. On June 6, 1981, he is ordained a priest.

He is immediately assigned to the new mission which P.I.M.E. has opened in Papua New Guinea. He is enthusiastic with this destination, happy to be one of the first missionaries in a new area.

In October of the same year, he goes to the United States to study English and remains there until the summer of the following year. Back in Italy, he learns that there are difficulties in obtaining the visa for Papua New Guinea, and while waiting he settles at P.I.M.E.'s minor seminary in Sotto il Monte. He stays there for a year and his confreres remember him as simple and humble, open to everyone; reserved, but constantly in search of authentic contacts with the people. He loves to go into the mountains and often climbs nearby Mt. Canto to meet with an old hermit who has lived alone there for years. He brings him cheese, bread, a bottle of wine.

Finally, tired of waiting for a departure that seems like it will never come, he asks his superiors for a change of assignment. He is open to any destination, except for the United States, the huge size of which intimidates him: "The country is big, the cities are big," he writes to his friend Letizia, "and also the people, who seem to have assimilated themselves to this great size, do everything in a big way." Tullio prefers a mission among simple people, with whom he can talk in a simple way, as with his own villagers of Mantua. He dreams of a rural mission, with fields and forests, contact with nature and with humble farmers. Difficulties and sufferings do not frighten him.

He is assigned to the Philippines, where the P.I.M.E. missionaries work in the poorest and most isolated areas of Mindanao, the least evangelized island of the country, with a large number of Muslims and tribal animists.[1]

---

[1] The tribal populations (about two million today) were present before the major immigration from Malaysia. There are several groups. In Mindanao they are called Lumad or Sebuani, which means "people of the river." Traditionally, they live in the forest, and when this is cut by the big lumber companies, they retreat to ever more remote and poor areas. They are in danger of extinction, as they resist integration into the national community, something the government desires.

On June 12, 1984, Fr. Tullio arrives in Tulunan, a small city called "the capital of terror" because of land wars and the presence of communist guerrillas; torture and even cannibalism are common. It is here that Fr. Tullio is called to carry out his mission, assisting Fr. Peter Geremia:

> The area where we work is flat, cultivated with rice, and stretching for ten kilometers up to the surrounding hills, where corn and sugar cane are grown. The land belongs to small farmers who are able to survive without large incomes. Most of the people work the fields. The methods of farming are rudimentary: there are no tractors or machines. On the hills there is no irrigation, so the harvest always depends on the weather. The roads are passable with a motorcycle. The rectory is made of wood, and we have electricity only during the day. Thus, in the evenings, when necessary, we use a lantern.

It is a difficult life. Because of the general situation of the Philippines and especially of Mindanao, life is marked

> …by economic crises, strong political tensions between the opposition and the ruling class, general discontent with the dictatorial system, fear among the common people, whose homes are routinely searched by the military, with subsequent arrests for joining the rebels or harboring them; imprisonment, deportation, and frequent cases of killings after arrest, without any trial; impunity for the military executioners, who carry out their suppression with government protection, flaunting all civil law and the most basic human rights. The church is united with all of these sad cases and raises its voice in protest, in defense of the oppressed. Often the poor and defenseless find their only support and advocate in the church, which acts with great difficulty and little result,

since it is confronting powers which are too strong and corrupt. We try to be signs of hope and promoters of justice... An entire overhaul of society is needed, and this takes a lot of time, through education in human values, the fundamental rights of every person, and justice. Certainly, this is one of our goals as priests.

Thus Tullio discovers his role as a priest. He who had questioned himself for years rediscovers the value of the presence of a missionary, for the growth of the people of God.

The areas assigned to P.I.M.E. are poor, mostly rural, isolated because of the difficulty in transportation and communication. Our pastoral work is carried out among people of the most humble conditions, and our own lifestyle tends to conform to the simple and essential style of the common people. For a Westerner to do this constitutes a strong evangelical witness. It is precious to the Filipinos themselves because such a lifestyle is a matter of *choosing* to live this way, thus, not just accepting the fate of an unchosen condition. I can see that the priest plays an important role and that the people expect much of him. He is a person to whom they come with every kind of need and necessity. I pray that I might be able to feel ever more a part of the lives and journey of these people, sorely tried by suffering. I thank all the people the Lord has given me to help me as I begin this mission.

Besides the difficult socio-political situation, Fr. Tullio must also face the problem of learning a new language and culture.
In a letter of December 17, 1984 he writes:

I'm getting used to the rhythm of Philippine life, which often tries my patience. Schedules are not respected, activities never begin when they are planned. There is not the least concern about the time which is wasted. It could be that the slowness of Philippine time is due to the heat, or insufficient food, or lack of motivation, or the isolation in which they live. I'm speaking about our mostly rural, poor, and underdeveloped area. Since I'm an antsy kind of person, I must constantly renew my openness to other cultures. In conversation, they engage in long discourses before ever getting to the point of the issue. It's difficult to understand what they are really thinking. Certain areas of their life remain a mystery to me. They don't like to express their opinions. I find myself in a state of general disorientation, due to the impact of a bare and essential reality and a world which I do not possess, but am just starting to enter into.

What bothers him the most is to see the malnutrition of the children who run to meet him as he enters a village, crying out, "Father!" They continually remind him that too many die without ever having lived. "The first time that I celebrated a funeral for a child a few months old, I was so touched with emotion that I could hardly finish the Mass." In time, his reflections on death become more profound:

I'm not saying that I've gotten used to it, but the acceptance of death, so common among the Filipinos, becomes less dramatic than for us; it is a normal event, a part of human existence, of which we need to be aware and for which we need to be prepared. Life and death intertwine as a matter of daily experience and give a more true and realistic awareness of our own mortality. It turns us away from our pretenses and vainglorious pursuits and teaches us a sense of limitation and thankfulness. Our life is a gift, which we have been given to carry out, but never to possess.

In one of his last letters to his friend, Fr. Gilberto Orioli, on March 27, 1985, Tullio writes:

…there's nothing else for me but to immerse myself in

this world and walk alongside these people, in fraternal communion and sharing. There is a lot of work to do and the assignment entrusted to us is great; but we are not alone. There is One who encourages us and strengthens us in our weakness. So, courage! Let's always remind one another of this.

In the meantime, the situation becomes more and more difficult. From the time of his arrival on Mindanao, Fr. Favali has sensed the tension in which the people live and he asks himself how much longer they can carry on with resignation.

There is a limit to patience, and no one can predict what will happen when the people truly become aware of their own rights. The situation is critical. Everyone is pushing for change. But of what kind, in what direction? There are those who expect radical change through armed revolution, by indiscriminate shedding of blood and the cost of too many human lives. Others want a gradual change, through constitutional and diplomatic means, in a more peaceful and less violent way. The future is uncertain. We hope that whatever happens, the growth of the people will be respected. God help us and bless us.

Meanwhile, the people of Tulunan are living in terror.

It all started with the "land wars" of 1972, a fierce and cruel battle which depopulated the area. By 1980 there are no houses anymore; all have been burned or destroyed. At this same time, the *Ilaga* cult is established, making Tulunan the most dangerous area in the diocese of Kidapawan. The *Ilagas* arm themselves against the Muslims, who have been killing the Christians like rats (thus the name chosen by the cult: *Ilaga,* which means "rat"). At first, they defend the villages and lands of the Christians, but then they begin to commit atrocities and tortures of their own. To make themselves brave and invincible, they even engage in acts of cannibalism. These groups become more and more uncontrollable, especially when the army uses them to create the Civilian Home Defense Forces (CHDF), to defend the population not only from the Muslims but also from the communist guerrillas. The CHDF, armed and protected by the military, attempt to take charge of the area. Since the communist guerrillas, hiding in the mountains and the forest, are hard to capture, they begin to attack those "suspected of communism" — priests, sisters, and Catholic lay people who have always defended the poor and also the Muslims when they were victims of injustice.

The atmosphere, then, is full of hate and violence, and little is needed to set off tragic events.

In Tulunan, the clan of the Manero brothers, ex-*Ilaga,* who hold a reign of terror in the area, threatens the "communist priests" and speak of "killing an Italian." The army makes use of these men for its dirty work: intimidation, torture, and summary execution of political adversaries. The missionaries live in daily fear, but their faith allows them to carry on in spite of everything and to stand by their people, in whom every day they rediscover the face of Christ. In this context, Fr. Peter Geremia, an Italo-American P.I.M.E. priest and confrere of Tullio, distinguishes himself for his astute actions and penetrating Christian message.

The killings and disappearances increase, but astride his Honda, Tullio arrives at every village in his pastoral care, always smiling, always available and ready to help.

Holy Week of 1985 brings rich celebrations and meetings in which the Christians participate with devotion. On April 11, a paramilitary group gathers on the main road of La Esperanza, a neighboring village to Tulunan. There are 15 of them, armed to the teeth and led by the Manero brothers, who live nearby.

As is their habit, they spend a couple of hours drinking and shouting. Then they pull out a manifesto with a list of names. These are the people they accuse of harboring communist guerrillas. Among others are the names of Fr. Geremia, the companion of Fr. Tullio, and a certain Rufino Robles, who happens to be passing by at that very moment. They begin shooting, and Robles seeks refuge in a nearby house. The armed thugs surround the house, howling and shooting in the air. Someone hurries to the parish with a note: "Father, help, at La Esperanza."

Fr. Tullio has just returned from a baptism celebration, because Fr. Geremia has gone to visit other barrios. Without any hesitation, he fires up the motorcycle and speeds to the place. He is able to enter the house and examine Robles' wounds for a few moments. Then he suddenly hears more gunfire outside. Tullio goes to the window and sees one of the Maneros opening fire on his motorcycle. He goes out of the house, even though the others are pleading with him to stay put. "They won't do anything to me," he says resolutely.

Edilberto Manero greets him on the street with a laugh. "Father," he shouts, "do you want to wrestle?"

Tullio holds up his hands with his palms outstretched to indicate that he comes in peace. Unarmed, seeking dialogue as he has for his whole life, he approaches the rifle-bearing man. Edilberto fixes his gaze on him and then shoots him in the chest. Tullio falls on his knees and he is shot again. The missionary is already dead, but the whole gang continues to shoot at him, laughing and whistling, repeatedly stomping his body as they dance and sing.

At sunset, Fr. Geremia returns home. Some of his parishioners have pleaded with him to take a different route than usual, without saying why, but he knows that the paramilitary unit is looking for him to carry out their sentence of death. At the parish he finds the note asking for help, but Tullio is not there. He runs to the police station, trying to get two policemen to go with him; they are terrified too. A half hour later, he reaches the ravaged body of his confrere, laying in the deserted street. He kneels down and, weeping, begins to pray.

Even though the Maneros have killed Fr. Tullio in order to give a lesson to the priests and to intimidate the Christians of the entire diocese of Kidapawan, three thousand people come to attend the funeral of Fr. Tullio Favali. They are witnesses once again to the fact that in Christ, death brings life, and that hate cannot kill love.

FR. SALVATORE CARZEDDA

(DECEMBER 20, 1943 – MAY 20, 1992)

> Sometimes it's very difficult and mysterious to discover
> the way in which God is leading us. Now we are living
> like Abraham … we will go to a land we do not know.
> We don't even know the name of this land: Thailand,
> Africa, Japan, Philippines, Hong Kong? Right now, I
> don't even want to know. We'll send you a postcard
> with the address after we get there.

It is October 19, 1975. Fr. Salvatore Carzedda is writing from
Oxford to a group of young people in Mascalucia (Sicily). He feels very
close to them, just as he is united in friendship with the two confreres
who are with him to study English before leaving for the missions.
Sebastiano D'Ambra, Antimo Villano and Salvatore are an inseparable
trio. During the four years that they served together in Mascalucia,
they grew every day in mutual respect, esteem, and love.

It is just after his ordination on July 15, 1971 that Fr. Salvatore is
assigned together with his classmate, Fr. Antimo, to Mascalucia where
Fr. Sebastiano is already stationed. Here, the three missionaries, well
aware of the continuing struggle in which young people are engaged, a
struggle which came to a head in the violent demonstrations of the late
sixties, dedicate themselves to forming a vocational community, by
which to reintroduce to the youth the beauty of the faith and of the
missionary ideal. Fr. Salvatore is a charismatic figure: he knows how to
listen, to instill confidence, to share his deep hopes.

It is a lot of work, but the positive results are worth it. Nevertheless, after just three years, they ask the superiors for a mission assignment, because they know that in order to live out their ideals fully, they must leave everything, even that which brings them great satisfaction.

The first to leave Mascalucia is Salvatore, who goes to London to study English. It is his first experience of loneliness. On the evening of November 6, 1974, he is especially homesick for his friends in Sicily, as he writes to one of them:

> I miss you a lot. I feel more and more empty each day, and I think back with longing to the grace-filled time we spent together. I am living my "desert" experience. The study of English, as intense as it is, does not bring much satisfaction. I am impatient to be able to speak, but it takes time to really understand and dialogue with others. I go to school every day. It is a great drudgery, but I pray that everything is working to serve the Kingdom of God within me… Sometimes I really do feel like Abraham: alone, not knowing what my life will be like.

After a year in England, Salvatore is joined by Antimo and Sebastiano. But their final destinations are still a mystery. Then, finally, in January of 1977, the superiors announce their decision. The three friends are assigned to the Philippines.

Salvatore and Sebastiano are appointed to the mission of Siocon: "Siocon is truly desolate," Fr. Sal writes two months after his arrival.

> It is a town north of Zamboanga, on the island of Mindanao. The parish extends for 4000 square kilometers. You can reach the area only by sea, because there are no roads. You take a type of ship, and if everything goes well, after 10 or 15 hours on the ocean, you transfer to smaller boats which take you into shore. Remember the movie about Fr. Damien? It's exactly the same! Except it's one thing to see it on film and another to really live through it! To reach the twenty villages in our care, we go by foot, or sometimes by small boats. There is no

electricity and no telephone. Mail arrives about once a week when that famous conveyance, the *Lancia*, sails from Zamboanga.

But here in Siocon we are really lucky, because the mail is delivered right to our rooms. The postman, when he is not working (which is most of the time, to tell you the truth), is always at our house.

I'm a little bit bothered by the isolation here, but the people are poor, open, and welcoming, not yet touched by consumerism. After a lot of prayer and reflection we have chosen this place as our field of work … thus, a small motor boat has brought me and Sebastiano to the "center of the world."

In Siocon, Fr. Sal dreams of working with the youth, as he did in Mascalucia. But first, he has to dedicate himself to the training of catechists and church leaders. The vast parish needs well prepared lay people to lead the liturgical services and community life of the villages. "Little by little, as time goes by," he writes on December 4, 1978, "everything is becoming more familiar: the faces of so many people, the problems of the poor, the language, the customs, the traditions."

We understand more and more that, in spite of appearances, we live in a different world! The political and economic situation of the Philippines is well known by now. We continue to live under the military regime and martial law, and it seems that the system is just getting stronger!

In general, the people are afraid; they stay quiet and continue to suffer and be exploited. In our area, road development, electricity, some small industries, are no more than a dream. This is Siocon: cut off from the rest of the world and from the commercial and administrative centers of Mindanao. The people live on what they can produce. They eat rice, vegetables, and fish. Rice and fish, three times a day, every day. Time passes quickly and we are becoming more and more aware of the purpose of our presence here among these people. There are many things which could be done, but essentially we are here to testify to Gospel values and to announce liberation from every form of slavery!

In 1979, Fr. Antimo arrives in Siocon, to take the place of Fr. Sebastiano, who begins to work more directly with the Muslims. It is a critical and tension-filled time. The Muslim guerrillas are particularly active in their struggle for the independence of Mindanao from the central government of Manila.

The situation is becoming more and more serious, and may soon be out of the control of Marcos, who rules the country with military strength and "presidential decrees." The whole life of the people, the fruit of their fields and their labor, their free time, education, socio-economic development, even the use of what little property they own, all depend upon "presidential decrees"! Terror reigns supreme; the people stay quiet in the face of military abuses, because they fear reprisals.

The three friends devote themselves to different types of work, but always in a spirit of mutual support. They meet often to talk about their experiences, their impressions, and reflections. Fr. Sebastiano tells them: "I have known so many young Muslims who speak with determination of armed struggle, violence, and revolution as the only solution for recovering their rights." Salvatore listens, fascinated by the world his friend is exploring. "So many times," Sebastiano continues, "I have listened in silence to their stories, especially since I have gone to live in a Muslim village by the sea."

In the evenings, close to my hut, the youngsters gather to play, and the old folks come to tell their stories. There are many young men who feel the duty to protect their families, their traditions, their dignity, and their land. They've witnessed many acts of violence;

some of their relatives have been victims of massacres on the part of the military or feuds between Muslims and Christians. They know that they are obliged, according to their culture, to avenge them. It becomes almost a moral imperative.

You know, Sal, the other day I had a really frightening experience! I was with about 70 rebels and some of their families members in a place near the sea, far from the eyes of everyone, acting as a mediator of peace in some difficult negotiations. The beautiful landscape of the area did nothing to alleviate the tension, the lack of food and other discomforts. We stayed there a week. Then suddenly an alarm was raised. The military of the area was informed of our location. We were practically surrounded.

There was only one means of escape: through the forest and up a mountain. The rebel leader approached me with visible concern and said: "Father, we have been betrayed; the military is advancing and we have to leave this place at once. You go to the village and we'll head for the forest." But I didn't feel like I could leave them in this situation, so I said, "I'll come with you." Moved, he embraced me and said, "Father, if the military attacks us, we will defend you. You will be the last to die."

Salvatore remains close to his friend and encourages his efforts. Sebastiano is not the type to be intimidated, and after an adventure filled year, he has almost completed his mission of peace.

In the tranquil evenings of the dry season, while the cool breeze blows away the heat of the day and wafts through the large banana leaves, and the sun gives way to a myriad of stars, the two missionaries fire up their motorcycle and go to visit the tribal families spread throughout the forest. Going along the muddy paths, they have time to recount the happenings of the day, to discuss what needs to be done, until they finally return to their home, built of coconut wood.

On the night of February 9, 1981, they have reached the small village square. It is dark, the only light coming from paraffin lamps in the windows of the huts and the cloud covered reflection of the moon. Suddenly, while a group of people gather around the motorcycle to speak with the fathers, there is a pistol shot. A young tribal falls to the ground, dead. But the target is clearly "the priest."

Thus begins a situation which becomes increasingly unbearable. Fr. Salvatore continues his pastoral work, but Fr. Sebastiano has to leave Siocon and go back to Italy. They have seen with their own eyes that when engaging in dialogue it is not enough to talk, to be sympathetic, to have many friends; it also requires personal sacrifice, taking up one's cross, learning how to wait.

Thus, while Salvatore concentrates his efforts on creating good relations with the Muslims and tribals, Sebastiano enrolls at the Pontifical Institute of Arab and Islamic Studies in Rome, never losing hope that he will return to the Philippines one day.

His hope is not in vain. In 1983, he arrives once again in Mindanao and immediately sets about to realize his dream. In Zamboanga City, he founds a movement of Muslim-Christian dialogue called *Silsilah* ("Chain"). It is a group of Christians and Muslims who meet to deepen their faith and friendship through prayer, reflection, exchange of ideas, and gestures of solidarity. Little by little the project grows, involving more and more people.

Fr. Salvatore, from Siocon, continues to support the initiative of his friend in prayer, and follows the first steps with great interest. However, in 1986, he is assigned to a new position:

> I've received a call from Rome and a new destination in the United States, where I've been asked to work in formation and missionary awareness. So, at the most beautiful moment of my missionary life, I must leave everything and start all over again. What do you think of that, Sebastiano?

Once more he asks the advice of his friend, who in the meantime has been elected Regional Superior of the Philippines. Sebastiano, who knows very well how hard it is to enter a completely new environment after leaving loved ones and cherished activities, and also how much Sal's presence in the Philippines is needed, could appeal to keep him there. But he also understands that it would not be right to make a decision based on purely human motives, and he encourages him to go, proposing that he take advantage of his time in the U.S.A. to deepen his study of interreligious dialogue. "And, who knows, when you return here, maybe we can collaborate more closely with Silsilah! Wouldn't it be great to work together again, you and I?"

With his studies, pastoral commitments, and involvement with Filipino groups, the three years in Chicago fly by. Soon he finds himself with Sebastiano once again, right at the time when Cory Aquino, the new president of the Philippines, awards *Silsilah* the National Peace Award, in September of 1990. Fr. Salvatore is overwhelmed by the applause and official speeches, but his heart is filled with happiness. By April of the following year, he is working full-time in the movement in charge of publications: a monthly magazine and a series of formational booklets.

Meanwhile, the political and social situation of the Philippines continues to be difficult. Fr. Sal writes on Christmas day 1990:

> In view of the indifference of politicians and the armed violence of those in power, the dreams of the poor are turned into nightmares of the struggle to survive! In the midst of such confusion and disregard for life, we continue to work for peace through the slow process of dialogue... It is only in dialogue that we ourselves are enriched and able to enrich others with our religious experience.

And a year later:

> We continue to proclaim hope, convinced that our own transformation and that of the world is not the immediate effect of a single decision or historical event,

but a commitment for every day of our lives. The experience of dialogue is placed in this context of hope which goes beyond the daily frustrations. If we give up dialogue we will lose the ability to imagine a world different than this one; we will lose the ability to imagine methods of endurance and means of mutual support in the long struggle for justice and truth; we will lose the ability to hope and love in every way. I believe our endurance is an act of joy, because it is an act of hope in the One who has conquered death.

Thus, in spite of the difficulties, the work of *Silsilah* proceeds, and Salvatore devotes himself to summer courses on Muslim-Christian dialogue.

It is the evening of May 20, 1992. After the successes of the previous year, Salvatore and Sebastiano are again offering the summer courses to young Christians and Muslims. The first day of the course has just finished and the missionaries, who up to that day had been uncertain about how the initiative would be received, are quite satisfied and congratulate one another on a job well done. They exchange a few more ideas and then, while Sebastiano stays to set up for the next day, Salvatore heads home by car. "See you tomorrow!"

Those last words are still reverberating when Salvatore's car, by now close to the P.I.M.E. residence, is overtaken by one of two motorcycles which have been following him for some time. Pulling alongside, the driver shoots a pistol several times at the missionary.

Fr. Sebastiano recalls:

I was called immediately to the scene of the crime, and I saw Sal in a pool of blood. He was already dead." Strong feelings passed through my mind and heart. I was there, speechless, next to my best friend, a martyr of dialogue.

It seemed unreal. He would never speak to me again … it seemed like everything was finished. He often told me that true dialogue is found in listening and in silence. I laughed when he said that, because he was such a chatterbox. Now everything is silence for him. It is, however, the eloquent silence of martyrdom.

The Christians and Muslims who came by the hundreds to pray at his coffin have expressed the will to continue the path of dialogue, with even more commitment, sure that Fr. Salvatore is guiding our way from heaven. And this is true.

But who killed Fr. Salvatore?

"I've asked myself that question so many times since that day in May," Fr. Sebastiano continues.

The situation is complicated, and even today it's difficult to make a complete analysis of what happened. Some say it was Muslim fundamentalists, others think it was the military, and still others believe it was some persons or groups who want to stop the path of peace and dialogue between Muslims and Christians. What is the truth? I still wonder myself. I only know one thing for sure: that we must carry on. There is a new bond of commitment, a pact of blood, which no one can tear from my heart. In the midst of this mystery, there is the challenge to work together in order to find the way of harmony and peace.

AFTERWORD

MARTYRDOM IN THE LIGHT OF THE GOSPEL

By Fr. Bruno Maggioni

THE NEW TESTAMENT RECOUNTS THREE EPISODES OF MARTYRDOM: the beheading of John the Baptist (Mk. 6:17–29), the stoning of Stephen (Acts 7:55–60), and the crucifixion of Jesus. The first is the prefiguration of Jesus' martyrdom, and the second is the shadow which follows it. At the center, then, is the crucifixion. It is in light of the martyrdom of Jesus that we can discover — all in one place and with extreme clarity — the traits of Christian martyrdom: its meaning, purpose, and direction. For this reason, I have chosen the cross as the guiding criterion of our discussion, convinced that there is not any other height which offers so great a view. Only if it is superimposed upon the crucifixion does Christian martyrdom reveal its astonishing originality. The cross of Jesus is the normative principle to discern the truth about Christian martyrdom.

A second necessary reference point for our discussion is the New Testament theme of testimony. This is suggested by the fact that "martyr" and "martyrdom" are transliterations of two Greek terms (*martys* and *martyria*), which mean precisely "witness" and "testimony."

From the Old Testament to the New Testament, up to the first decades of the early church, there is a continual evolution of the term *martys*. It passes progressively from a generic concept of a witness to a fact, to a more precise meaning of witness to a truth, and finally to testimony given with the shedding of one's own blood.

It's not our purpose here to reconstruct the evolution of the word "martyr" in detail. What has been said is enough to indicate that martyrdom is a particular "figure" of testimony, a figure which, precisely because of its particularity, brings to the surface its profound traits, distinguishing it from any other form of evangelical witness. Not every testimony can be called martyrdom, because martyrdom includes the shedding of blood. But martyrdom, in whatever historical form it assumes, must always reflect its nature as testimony.

In the Synagogues and Tribunals

In His trial before Pilate, Jesus declares His identity solemnly and publicly with words which touch our theme directly: "You say that I am a king. For this I was born and for this I came into the world, to give *testimony* to the truth." (Jn. 18:37) This solemn declaration of Jesus tightly binds, under the category of testimony *(martyrein),* the cross which is to come and His entire mission which has come before, the tension of the entire life of Jesus and the reason for His death. It is a declaration of rare density, which requires an attentive examination.

Jesus makes His declaration in the course of a trial; thus, the testimony is taking place where it belongs, in a court of law. To testify is a verb which has the flavor of legal proceedings. In the New Testament, this reference, explicit or assumed, is never absent. It is predicted to the disciples that they will be handed over to tribunals and synagogues, arraigned before governors and kings, "for my sake, as a witness before them and the pagans." (Mt. 10:17–18) John's Gospel in particular presents the trial of Jesus before Pilate in space and time, as a figure of an imaginary (and very real) trial which pervades the entire story, in which Jesus is the accused and the world is the accuser. A witness is the disciple who takes part in this trial placing himself or herself totally on the side of Jesus. Committing oneself wholly to the master, the disciple is under the same accusation and the same sentence.

It is this attitude which makes it "natural" and even "necessary" that martyrdom, in all its forms, follow the path of the church like a shadow. Martyrdom is the sign of the authenticity of a church, the irrefutable proof that it is saying the same things to the world that the crucified One has already said.

Before Governors and Kings

Testimony is a *public* fact. Jesus' testimony was before the Sanhedrin and Pilate; the disciples' testimony was before governors and kings. The violence which strikes a martyr is never, or only very rarely, perpetrated by a single individual; rather, it comes from a regime, a hostile power, a system. The deep reason for this public connotation of martyrdom is that the truth to which the martyr testifies is by its nature public. If the church were to close in on itself, martyrs would be very difficult to find. But would it still be church? Testimony becomes martyrdom only when the proclamation of the Gospel touches and threatens collective, cultural, social, and political idolatry. It's not that martyrs are politicians; it's simply that they proclaim, as Jesus did to Pilate, the kingship of the one God.

In the words of Jesus to the Roman magistrate, "kingship" and "truth" almost overlap. (Jn. 18:37) Kingship speaks immediately of the public character of the truth which Jesus has come to testify. The preceding passage underlines the "novelty" and "difference" of the kingship which Jesus vindicates: "My kingdom is not of this world." (18:36) Christ's kingship has another origin; he has another loyalty, another worldview. It is based not in the defense of self but in the giving of self, not in submission to the role of the state but in total loyalty to the truth, not in violence but love. If Jesus had testified to a truth which was limited to the private sphere, He never would have been crucified. Neither would He have been crucified if He had affirmed His kingship according to the world's way of thinking. It is the *difference* of His kingship which disturbed, and continues to disturb, the world. (Jn. 15:18–19) The true reason that the hatred of the world is directed toward Jesus and His disciples is always the perception of a difference in origin and loyalty, the irritation of facing an obedience to the truth which escapes its own grasp. The world cannot recognize itself in gratuitous and universal love — which is the profound truth to which Jesus came to testify — but only in competition and power. For this reason the world is uncomfortable with people who do not pursue their own interests and thus it rejects them, resorting to lies, threats, or both.

The two powers of politics and religion were set against Jesus, and *together* — even though they were hardly allies under normal circumstances — they condemned him. Religion and politics are two profound needs of humanity, but it is precisely in each of them that idolatry can arise, in every age. On the one hand, the truth of Jesus threatened the theocratic system and thus upset the religious world; and on the other hand, that same truth threatened the absolutism of the state, upsetting the political world. So we can easily understand that the martyrdom of Jesus came as a result of a mixture of religious and political motives. And the same is true today, perhaps more than ever, for many Christian martyrs. But this mixture of religion and politics does not dim the purity of evangelical martyrdom; on the contrary, it manifests the truth of it.

Knowing What Is Going to Happen

I have insisted on the public character of martyrdom, I think, with good reason. Nevertheless, martyrdom is above all an essentially interior and personal event, a free and knowledgeable choice. Recounting the arrest of Jesus, the Gospel of John notes that He was "fully aware of what was about to happen to Him." (18:4) Jesus is not overwhelmed by force; He gives himself up. Seen from the outside, the arrest is an act of violence against Jesus; but seen from within His soul, it becomes a free surrender. The two points of reference show the two faces of martyrdom: violence and gift.

Martyrdom is determined inside the witness, in the "heart" — the Bible would say — where one chooses one's own way of living, or what position one takes before God, others, and oneself. Testimony to the truth, as Jesus understands it, is much more than a simple proclamation of the truth, even if it is made publicly. The verb "testify" implies devotion, loyalty, involvement of the whole self, accepting the fullest consequences. Such devotion makes the difference between Pilate and Jesus. Pilate can publicly and repeatedly declare the innocence of Jesus, but this is not testimony, because Jesus is not the truth to which he dedicates his life. For him, the power of the state is what is important. He is at the service of the emperor, not of God.

The martyr, instead, considers the kingship of Jesus not as *a* truth, but as *the* truth, the only truth of his or her life, that which stands above any other interest. These few observations should be enough to demonstrate that there is a strict continuity between one's life choice and martyrdom, between one's daily lifestyle and martyrdom. On the one hand, we have to remember that it is not through suffering that a martyr becomes a witness; a martyr suffers because he or she is *already a witness.* On the other hand, we must be equally aware that it is precisely in suffering and dying that the martyr demonstrates the truth and fullness of his or her witness.

For this reason, martyrdom is not an interruption of life, but the conclusion; it is not a broken, silenced, unfinished testimony, but a testimony brought to fullness.

What transforms a violent death into martyrdom is the *truth* witnessed to by the one who submits to violence, not the intention of the one who commits the act. Most of the time, the violence which strikes the witness is the result of wickedness and idolatry. But it can also be, paradoxically, the result of a distorted but totally sincere attempt to "give glory to God," as we read in the Gospel of John: "The hour is coming when anyone who kills you will think he is giving worship to God." (16:2) But it is not these different circumstances which qualify Christian martyrdom. The central point is that, in every case, the witness is struck down because he or she affirms the kingship of God.

Jesus went to the cross freely and knowingly and approached the moment of His death with full awareness. But it's not always like that, and it's not necessary that it be. A martyr, like any other person, can be brought to a completely unexpected death, which does not allow for any immediate or specific awareness. Yet, the martyr's death remains just as *free.* What makes the death a free offering — to God and others — is not necessarily the awareness of the moment but the free choice of a lifestyle which has brought one to that death. The free gift of dying is contained within an earlier freedom, that of having chosen a "dangerous" lifestyle, exposed to opposition and violence. The martyr does not choose death, but a way of life, a life like that of Jesus.

Martyrdom and Discipleship

Even if some traits have already been mentioned, I think it is opportune to delve more deeply into the relationship between martyrdom and Christian commitment. Martyrdom is a natural part of the Christian commitment. The form in which martyrdom comes may be exceptional, but the internal structures are already present in discipleship and mission.

You cannot follow Jesus "from a distance," as Peter tried to do in the impossible attempt to separate his destiny from that of the Master. Certainly, not every disciple *in fact* becomes a martyr, but all true discipleship carries the possibility of it. Indeed, martyrdom is a gift which God gives to a few, but the willingness to testify up to the fullest consequences is part of the normal structure of the disciple. The Gospels are very insistent upon this point. Discipleship requires, in every case, the denial of oneself, the acceptance of the cross, and the willingness to turn life itself upside down, not being concerned about preserving it, but choosing to give it up. (Mt. 8:34–35) The beatitude dealing with persecution is the only one repeated twice, and this alone indicates its importance. (Mt. 5:10–12) The first time it speaks of persecution "for the sake of justice" and the second time "for my sake." It is significant how the two formulations overlap.

I have spoken of profound structures which constitute evangelical discipleship and which are made more transparent in martyrdom. The two most important are: entrusting oneself to God and giving of oneself. These are the two tensions in the life of Jesus, which shine forth in particular splendor on the cross, so much so that even the high priests recognize them in the crucified One, even if they do so derisively: "He saved others, but he can't save himself." (Mt. 27:42) "He trusted in God, let God deliver him now, if he wants him." (Mt. 27:43)

Sometimes we read that the qualifying aspect of martyrdom is not faith, but love, even if — obviously — faith is not lacking. But is it so? In real life, faith and love stand or fall together. If there is a precedence, it is on the part of faith, which supports love and makes it possible. More than a gesture of love, martyrdom is an act of faith in the power of love (above all, that of God for His people), which in martyrdom is presented under the guise of silence and defeat.

Martyrdom and Mission

When He says, "For this I was born and for this I have come," Jesus is referring to His mission: not to this or that activity in particular, but to mission in its essence, in its root. The very word "testimony" implies a missionary direction. Testimony is always given not only in front of someone, but also directed toward someone: "as a witness before them and the pagans," Jesus tells his missionary disciples. (Mt. 10:18) The privileged place of testimony and martyrdom is the mission, the movement of the church outward.

Maybe the connection between martyrdom and mission is so obvious that we don't even have to dwell on it. But there is an aspect which is not always given due attention: martyrdom is a sign of the *effectiveness* of the mission, not simply its truth, nor only the sanctity of the missionary.

Because "they could not withstand the wisdom and the spirit with which he spoke," they decided to stone the deacon Stephen. (Acts 6:10) And because he "is performing many signs" Caiaphas makes the decision to condemn Jesus. (Jn. 11:47) What inspires the decisive action, therefore, is not a failed mission, but a successful one; not its weakness, but its strength; not words deprived of truth and conviction, but convincing words. Martyrdom is the result of truth, not falsehood; meekness, not violence.

The first missionaries were probably not bewildered in the face of persecution, both because they were supported by the memory of their Lord and because they had been trained in a religious tradition which already spoke much of martyrdom. They were well acquainted with the figure of the "just one" who was ready to die rather than transgress God's law. And above all, they knew that the prophets always suffered greatly for faithfulness to their mission. The prophet flatters neither the authorities nor the populace, and thus persecution always seems to be an inseparable, and natural, companion of his mission. Naturally the prophet is not condemned for his piety, but because his words create disruption. The accusation leveled against him is always: "Why do you disturb Israel?" (1 Kg. 18:17)

He Will Testify to Me

It is impossible to understand Christian martyrdom without an explicit reference to the Spirit. According to the synoptic tradition, the true bearer of testimony in the synagogues and tribunals, before governors and kings, is the Spirit: "For it will not be you who speak, but the Spirit of your Father speaking for you." (Mt. 10:20)

The discourse in the Gospel of John is even more explicit: "When the Advocate comes, whom I will send you from the Father ... he will testify to me, and you also will testify to me." (Jn. 15:26–27) According to the Johannine tradition, the Spirit's presence is guaranteed not so much to suggest to the disciples how and what they are to speak, but to convince them of the inconsistency of the world, in spite of its attractiveness and the weight of its power. The Spirit takes on the task of preserving the disciples from scandal at the moment in which their faith is put dangerously to the test. The Spirit places into the heart of the persecuted disciples the assurance that the crucified One is the victor. He does not necessarily free them from turbulence and fear, but He gives them a serenity which remains strong even in the midst of the turbulence. For this reason, we can understand that martyrdom is a gift of the Spirit.

Most likely John was not thinking of individual disciples, but of the group: a persecuted and troubled, yet faithful, community; a community (what does it matter if it's small?) which withstands the compelling solicitations and proposals of the world; a community which does not fall into the error of seeking power with the excuse that it will be used for the glory of God; a community which denounces the contradictions that take shape within its own womb. All of this is the testimony of the Spirit. Within this testimony of the Spirit, martyrdom finds its place, its reason, and its direction. Separated from all of this, martyrdom loses its Christian character. It would be the example of a hero but not the testimony of a church.

We can discover another trait of the link between the Spirit and martyrdom, perhaps the most profound one of all, in the account of Stephen's martyrdom. Reading this account, there is a sense that the miracle of the Spirit is not in the power He gives the martyr to face death, nor even in the heroism of the martyr himself, but rather in the kind of "transparency" which makes the martyrdom of the disciple a living memory, *today*, of Jesus' martyrdom. There is an almost perfect correlation between the martyrdom of Jesus and that of Stephen. The latter re-actualizes the former. It is in this capacity for transparency that the originality of Christian martyrdom lies.

The Church and Martyrdom

Different comments made above oblige us to shift our attention, if only briefly, from the martyr to the community. Martyrdom is by its nature an ecclesial event.

The accounts of the Acts of the Apostles show that persecution was a part of the normal daily life of the church. If Luke speaks of persecution directed toward individuals, it is because he considers them representative figures, expressions of the entire community. Persecution is not the response of the world to this or that single member of the community but to the mission of the community as such. In striking down Stephen, the intent is to strike down the community and, beyond the community, the Gospel of Christ. For this reason, the community recognizes itself in its martyrs: that is where the face of the Lord and the face of the community itself emerge. But for the same reason, martyrdom is also a message *for* the church, and often it is a disturbing spur. Recognizing itself in its martyrs, the church is re-called to be what it is: the living memory of the crucified Lord.

The church celebrates and represents the death of the Lord in the sacramental mystery of the Mass: "Every time you eat this bread and drink this cup, you proclaim the *death* of the Lord, until He comes." (1 Cor. 11:26) But the church must proclaim the death of the Lord also in the truth and in the concrete actions of its life. Certainly this occurs in ordinary, everyday life, as Luke suggests when he points out that the disciple must "take up his cross *every day.*" (9:23) But the church must also be *visible,* and martyrdom is the most visible memory of the crucified One, the closest form possible to the historical event of Jesus.

Styles of Martyrdom

In the course of human history, not everyone dies in the same manner. So too the death of martyrs is not always the same. There are martyrs who die heroically, and those who die in a more humble way, almost hidden. There are different styles of martyrdom.

A passage from Karl Rahner *(On the Theology of Death)* merits our consideration:

> If we define the figure of the martyr as one recalling the person of Christ, the martyrs of today are perhaps even more similar to the Lord than those in times past: the martyr who falls to the ground and is immobilized by his own weakness; the martyr who feels abandoned by God; the martyr who is counted among true criminals, almost indistinguishable from them; the martyr who is almost convinced that he is not a martyr; the martyr who can't, but still does accomplish that which goes far beyond his own power; the martyr who is chained, perhaps for his whole life, and thus condemned, dies an apparently simple bourgeois death.

The surprising thing is that some of these styles have already been delineated by the evangelists in their accounts of the crucifixion, almost to tell us that Jesus has anticipated them in himself. One can die with a cry and question, like the Jesus of Mark and Matthew; or with a prayer of serene abandonment, like the Jesus of Luke; or with sovereign majesty, like the Jesus of John.

The martyr is not lessened by a common form of death. He or she can die as anyone dies. What transforms the death into martyrdom is something else.

Icon of Christ

Superimposed upon the crucified One, the Christian martyr represents the face of the evangelical God, which is not a formless face, dissolved in some vast universality, but a face which is revealed in the martyrdom of Jesus with precise, concrete traits all His own: the traits of a God who gives Himself. The cross is not only the icon of a martyr who dies for His God, but also the icon of the Son of God, who dies for humanity. This is the absolute novelty of the martyrdom of Jesus, and this is the novelty of Christian martyrdom which is in His memory.

"Lord, why can't I follow you now? I will give my life for you," Peter says to Jesus. (Jn.13:37) Peter's will is very sincere, yet inadequate, and I would say not yet Christian, for two reasons. First, Peter must understand that it is only *after* Jesus does so that he can, in his turn, give his life, because the disciple's gift of self is the fruit of the cross — the fruit and the response, not something that precedes or accompanies it. In order for the disciple to give his life, Jesus must first trace the steps and conquer the world. (Jn. 16:33) The martyrdom of the disciple is a following, not an accompaniment.

The second reason, even more important, is that Peter must correct the direction of his willingness to give his life —not only *for* Jesus, but *like* Jesus. That is, he must be willing to give for others, exactly like a shepherd who gives his life for his sheep (Jn. 10:11) As I have already indicated, this is what makes Christian martyrdom different for Jesus and for His disciples. A martyr is the memory of God's love for His people, not only an heroic example of one's devotion to God. It is the icon of God's love which comes down to us, not only that of the response of the person which goes up to Him. For this reason, martyrdom is not only an example of devotion, but a *revelation* of God — as the crucified One. We can see, at this point, that the *horizontal* direction — as we often define it in simple terms — of the love which a martyr expresses is not something peripheral to martyrdom, but at the center; it is a decisive and qualifying trait, not one that is added on.

Icon of Humanity

Our meditation on martyrdom could close here, once again in front of the cross. But there is one more trait which I believe useful to address: that is, martyrdom is an event which confronts the human person, *every* person, re-proposing to them the question which is more disturbing than any other. On the one hand, a martyr is a strident example of the defeat of justice, a defeat so scandalous that it seems to rob history of any meaning. On the other hand, the martyr impresses and fascinates us because of the *freedom* with which he or she dies, and this is filled with meaning. The martyr dies *for a reason,* not just because every person is destined to die.